D1611593

THE CENTERS OF CIVILIZATION SERIES

Edinburgh in the Age of Sir Walter Scott

Edinburgh
in the
Age of
Sir Walter Scott

By Douglas Young

UNIVERSITY OF OKLAHOMA PRESS : NORMAN

Books by Douglas Young

Auntran Blads: An Outwale o Verses. Glasgow, 1943.
A Braird o Thristles: Scots Poems. Glasgow, 1947.
The Use of Scots for Prose. Greenock, 1949.
Chasing an Ancient Greek:
Discursive Reminiscences of an European Journey. London, 1950.
Scottish Verse, 1851–1951:
Selected for the General Reader. London, 1952.
Romanisation in Scotland: An Essay in Perspective.
Tayport, 1955.
Scotland's Story. Edinburgh, 1957.
The Puddocks: A Verse Play in Scots from the Greek of
Aristophanes. Tayport, 1958.
The Burdies: A Comedy in Scots Verse from the Greek
of Aristophanes. Tayport, 1959.
Theognis. Leipzig, 1961.
Edinburgh in the Age of Sir Walter Scott. Norman, 1965.

The paper on which this book is printed bears the University of Oklahoma Press watermark and has an effective life of at least three hundred years.

Library of Congress Catalog Card Number: 65–24199

Copyright 1965 by the University of Oklahoma Press, Publishing Division of the University. Composed and printed at Norman, Oklahoma, U.S.A., by the University of Oklahoma Press. First edition.

For Charles Everett Kern II,

seventh-generation Washingtonian, in memory of
happy days in Washington, D.C., and Scotland.

Preface

LIKE THE GREEKS AND THE JEWS, the Scots have been influential beyond their national homeland, and out of proportion to their numbers. Scotsmen founded the navies of the United States of America and of Russia, and the banks of England and of France. Half the Presidents of the United States have been of Scottish name or partly Scottish descent, as have half the Prime Ministers of Great Britain for over a century. In the sciences and the arts, in literature and historiography, in the exploration of Africa and Australia and Canada, Scots were among the pioneers. But has there ever been a distinctive Scottish civilization? If so, where and when can it best be studied?

So far as Scotland has had a distinctive civilization, its most influential manifestation was surely in Edinburgh during the lifetime of Sir Walter Scott (1771–1832), a period that includes David Hume the philosopher, Adam Smith the economist, Robert Burns the poet, Robert Adam the architect, Henry Raeburn the painter, the English-language agents of

French Enlightenment associated with the first *Encyclopaedia Britannica,* the critics and reformers who wrote *The Edinburgh Review,* and an astonishing number of leading medical men, scientists, town planners, lawyers, churchmen, and others, whose activities focused on Edinburgh the attention of two generations of the English intelligentsia, and even of the French.

Physically, Scott's Edinburgh was thought by experienced tourists to be the most beautiful city in the world. A French traveler, Léon de Buzonnière, who saw it in 1827, thought that there was no spectacle in the universe more majestic and picturesque than the view from the middle of Princes Street. He found not a single modern building in bad taste, except for the tower commemorating the English Admiral Nelson, in what he termed "the anglo-saxon style." Mentally, the radiations from Edinburgh were extremely diverse, from the skepticism of Hume to the romanticism of Scott. The French and the Americans for decades made the Scottish philosophy of common sense the backbone of their academic teaching. That most shrewd of English observers of public affairs, Walter Bagehot, commented on Walter Scott's attitude to them with insight: "Anyone who studies the portions of the *Waverley* novels concerned with sociology and economics will be struck not only with a plain sagacity which we could equal in England, but with the digested accuracy and theoretical completeness which they show. There appears to be in the genius of the Scottish people—fostered no doubt by the abstract metaphysical education of their universities—a power of reducing human actions to formulae or principles."

Bagehot there stressed one aspect of the genius of the Scottish people, the same aspect that Robert Burns had in mind when he wrote of

> *douce folk that live by rule,*
> *Grave, tideless-blooded, calm, and cool*

in contrast to himself and others of

> *The hairum-scairum, ram-stam boys,*
> *The rattlin' squad.*

The often paradoxical multiformity of Scottish culture and character, and the ways in which disparate elements fused to flower in Scott's Edinburgh, are the themes of the following essays in interpretation. I was myself schooled in Edinburgh, and spent most of my life there before going to the universities of St. Andrews and Oxford; and have constantly been resorting to it ever since. Forty years ago I became an addict of Walter Scott, and a little later of David Hume; and my concern has largely been to put both of these great men in their local perspective. But they are only the most prominent figures in a crowded scene. In clarifying the data stored in decades of reading I feel specially obliged to my old Aberdonian Hellenist colleague, Mr. David Murison, the learned and judicious editor of the *Scottish National Dictionary;* but any novel emphasis in the present volume is my own.

Douglas Young

Tayport, Scotland
February 23, 1965

Contents

Edinburgh in the Age of Sir Walter Scott

1

The Historical Background

THE CULTURAL COMPLEXITY of Scott's Edinburgh, often paradoxical, can be understood only in a long historical perspective. But we need not go back before A.D. 84, when the federated Celtic peoples of what is now Scotland fought a strong Roman army led by Julius Agricola, father-in-law of the historian Tacitus, at Mons Graupius, probably the Meikle Balloch hill by the Pass of Grange between Keith and Huntly in northeast Scotland. The Romans claimed a victory, but withdrew to the south, and soon afterwards evacuated their strong fortress at Inchtuthill, on the Tay above Perth. For over two more centuries Roman armies from time to time sought to conquer these Celts, whose leading tribe were called "Caledonians"; and the Romans built two walls from sea to sea to cut them off from the tamed Britons in England and Wales to the south. Hadrian's Wall, from Tyne to Solway, was the effective frontier of the Roman province. Between it and the Antonine Wall, from Forth to Clyde, the

3

Romans had intermittent control, and the local tribes gradually became Christians after the conversion of the Emperor Constantine. The first known Christian was St. Nynia, a man of the Novantae tribe in southwest Scotland, who worked as a missionary bishop at Whithorn on the Solway from A.D. 397. At this period the Celts of south Scotland were styled "*Brittones*," often translated "Brythons." The unsubdued and still pagan tribes of the north were called by the Romans "*Picti*," "Painted Men" or "Tattooees," from their love of tattooing their skins. In their own language, a form of Welsh, these Celts probably called themselves something like "*Albani*," "Men of Alban," the slogan of the Picts at a battle in 1138. The name may be connected with "*Alp*," and refer to the hilliness of the country. The Picts were a pastoral people, herding cattle in swampy forests, and cultivating patches of grain. They were good horsemen, metalworkers, and carpenters; musical and convivial; and much given to fighting, as their fortified hill-towns indicate. But they normally combined to keep out imperial conquerors; and among themselves they seem to have had some system of law and arbitration, with the various local kings acknowledging a High King.

In the 360's a Roman historian tells of the Picts raiding the province of Britannia with Scots and Saxons. The Saxons came from the North Sea coasts of Germany, and later occupied the southeast of England, with their kindred Angles occupying the northern part of the east coast. The Scots were still in northeast Ireland, in a corner of Ulster, but anxious to extend across the narrow seaways. Ammianus Marcellinus describes them as *"per diversa vagantes,"* "wandering through various places"; and the Scots have been doing so ever since. Their native princes were called "Dal-Reti," or "Dalriata"; and about A.D. 500 one of them secured territory in mainland Scotland, on the Kintyre Peninsula projecting towards Ireland, as a vassal of the Pictish High King. In 563, St. Columba, a Scot from Donegal, Ireland, founded his monastery on the island of Iona, part of the Dalriata sub-kingdom in Pictland, and visited the High King of the Picts near Inverness. It seems that Christianity had already become known to the Picts, but Columba's Iona and its daughter-houses were powerful agencies in developing it. Columba belonged to the Gaelic intelligentsia of Ireland, the most learned men in Europe at that time, west of Constantinople; and his monastic movement brought in the Gaelic language, which gradually replaced among Brythons and Picts the older Welsh. It is a paradox that the earliest literature extant from Scotland is in Welsh, and the oldest Welsh literature extant is from what is now Scotland. The Teutonic Angles pressed in between Picts and Welsh, and overran Scotland up to the Forth. After a defeat by the Picts at Dunnichen in 685, the Angles declined. But the Picts faced a severer test from about 800, when Vikings from Denmark and Norway swarmed round the coasts, with a finer model of ship than any yet known. Norsemen took over Shetland, Orkney, and the Western Isles, and some coastal areas; but the bulk of the Pictish kingdom stood firm. In 843 the Scots subking Kenneth MacAlpin succeeded to the High Kingship of Pictland (called in Latin, *"Albania"*), partly having a claim through female descent, but largely through disposing of a military power trained in fighting Vikings, and with the support of the Columban church. The High Kingship remained in his family, and a Gaelic-speaking aristocracy consolidated the kingdom in the next two centuries, roughly to the present frontier of Scotland and England on the rivers Tweed and Sark.

In the mid–eleventh century there was a disputed royal succession, between Macbeth and Duncan, after which Duncan's heir, Malcolm III Canmore (1057–93), secured the throne with English and Danish assistance. It is significant that Macbeth (1040–57) was the only Scottish king to visit Rome, and a promoter of Latin studies; and that he employed a bodyguard of Norman cavalrymen, who died to a man for him. This period was the heyday of the Normans as the most efficient people in Europe, superb as horse-breeders and fighters, shipbuilders and sailors, castle-builders and churchmen, architects and administrators and organizers of governments. When Malcolm Canmore married, in 1070, the Anglo-Saxon heiress of Alfred the Great, now known as St. Margaret, she aided him in modernizing his Gaelic kingdom according to the fashionable European ideas. She had been reared in Hungary, where she was great-niece of the King St. Stephen, and at the court of her Anglo-Norman grand-uncle Edward the Confessor in England; she and her sons, especially David I (1124–53), brought in many colonies of French and English monks of various orders to Scotland, and encouraged the founding of burghs, fortified trading posts, often with Flemish or Anglic settlers. When William of Normandy conquered England in 1066, he harried Yorkshire, whence many Angles fled to Scotland; and Malcolm Canmore asserted his wife's claim to England as heiress of Alfred the Great. He seems to have claimed a Scottish frontier on Hadrian's Wall, perhaps implicitly admitted by the early Norman conquerors when they built fortresses at each end of it, Newcastle-on-Tyne (1080) and Carlisle (1092). As late as 1137, according to Ordericus Vitalis, the conquered English were detected in a conspiracy to murder all the occupying Norman master-race on one day, and thereafter make the Scots king David I king also of England. One recalls the massacre of St. Brice's Day (1002), an attempt to dislodge the earlier Danish conquerors. A cultural by-product of this political tangle was that Scots kings encouraged the use of the northern form of English, the Anglic of the old Northumbrian kingdom; and it became a public medium in the municipal law of the Scots burghs, mainly on the east coast, at a time when English in conquered England was becoming a neglected patois under the Normans. From this form of Northern Insular West Teutonic, or Anglic, developed the Court Scots of the medieval Scots parliament and law courts, sometimes called "Broad Scotch," or "*Lallans*" ("Lowland speech"), as found in the works of Burns and Scott.

Scottish civilization has never been a monoglot affair. Like the Jews and the Swiss, the Scots have used a plurality of tongues concurrently. In thirteenth-century Scotland one could have heard Gaelic over half the country, scraps of Welsh in the south, Norse round the coasts, and Scots in the southeast, and the burghs and monasteries. Clerics such as the internationally famous John Duns Scotus and Michael Scott would use Latin. Nobles, especially those interested in crusading, would have a working knowledge of Norman French. By 1250 about one-fifth of the land was owned by noble families brought in by St. Margaret's family, often of Norman origin, like the Bruces, Lindsays, Grahams, and Ramsays; or Bretons, like the Stewarts; or Flemings, like the Douglases and Murrays. But many of them held their lands through marriages with Celtic heiresses, and the bulk of the landowning class was of Celtic origin, whether Pictish or Scottish. Some were of Northumbrian Angle stock, like the Swintons, ancestors of Sir Walter Scott, or the Humes, from whom sprang David Hume the philosopher. As Edinburgh became a frontier capital near the most threatened frontier, the southeast, the Anglicizing elements thereabouts tended to grow, and the Gaelic heritage to decline. Celtic customs persisted, for instance in the inauguration ceremonies of the kings at Scone near Perth, as late as the crowning of Charles II in 1651. But the Celtic feudal system was modernized on an Anglo-Norman model, with titles registered in charters. The first recorded Scots Parliament was in 1173; the first held at Edinburgh was in 1215. By 1292, Edinburgh Castle was the main repository of the kingdom's archives. In modernizing the church, St. Margaret's influence developed organization by bishops, in place of powerful lay abbots; and the celibacy of the clergy was enforced. The dioceses, in order of wealth, were St. Andrews, possessing alleged bones of the Apostle, Glasgow, Aberdeen, Moray, Dunkeld, Dunblane, Brechin, Whithorn, Ross, Caithness, and Argyll. By a papal bull of 1192 the Scottish church was declared "a special daughter" of the Apostolic See, entirely free from subjection to English archbishops. The Scots bishops also resisted subjection to one another, and collaborated as colleagues, with an elected *Primus* or chairman. As an autonomous body, owning one-third or so of the land, this Scottish church was the backbone of the wars of independence forced on the nation by aggressions of the French kings of England, who exploited a disputed Scots royal succession in 1290. Besides the church, there was the constitutional concept of "the community of the kingdom of Scotland," fully formulated before the struggle began. Professor G. W. S. Barrow, in his epoch-making monograph *Robert Bruce,* writes: "At the very time that some of the most acute and radical of the political thinkers of western Europe were working out a theory of sovereignty, the community of the realm of Scotland was giving practical expression to such a theory, at first under its Guardians, finally under its king, Robert I. The political manifesto which we call the Declaration of Arbroath (1320) forms a practical counterpart to the famous work of theory which was its close contemporary, Marsiglio of Padua's *Defensor Pacis* of 1324."

In 1290 there were a dozen or so claimants to the Scots crown, with two principal claimants. By the principle of primogeniture, then becoming fashionable in Europe, John Baliol had the best claim, and Edward I of England, to whom all claimants submitted for arbitration, decided for Baliol in 1292. By the traditional Scots principle of reckoning a claim from proximity to the nearest common ancestor

of the deceased monarch, the best claim was that of Robert
Bruce, Lord of Annandale, which was backed by "the community of the realm," and by a body of grandees called the
Council of the Seven Earls. To avoid civil war, the Scots
acquiesced in the award to Baliol. When, however, the King
of England tried to treat him as a mere subking, or puppet,
the Scots rebelled, and made an alliance with France (1295),
which endured until 1560. Unprepared for war, Baliol's government was overthrown, and he himself captured; but at
once the Bishops and some of the magnates organized a
revolt, under two *Guardians,* or Regents, Sir William Wallace and Sir Andrew Moray. After various ups and downs,
old Bruce the Claimant's grandson, another Robert Bruce,
became king (1306–29), and carried the nation to victory at
Bannockburn in 1314. Six years after that, a group of parliamentary leaders appending seals, together with "the remain-
ing barons and free-holders, and the whole community of the
realm of Scotland," issued the Arbroath manifesto, rehears-
ing to the Pope, as chief international authority, the claim of
the Scots to national self-government. About King Robert
Bruce they say: "The divine providence, the right of succession by the laws and customs of the kingdom (which we will
defend till death), and the due and lawful consent and assent
of all the people, made him our king and prince. To him we
are obliged and resolved to adhere in all things, both upon
account of his right and his own merit, as being the person
who hath restored the people's safety in defence of their liberties. But, after all, if this prince shall leave these principles he
hath so nobly pursued, and consent that we or our kingdom

be subjected to the king or people of England, we will immediately endeavour to expel him as our enemy, and as the subverter both of his own and our rights, and will make another king who will defend our liberties. For, so long as there shall but one hundred of us remain alive, we will never consent to subject ourselves to the dominion of the English." The manifesto then adapts a phrase of Sallust: "It is not for glory, wealth, or offices, that we fight: it is for freedom alone, which no good man gives up except with his life." As a statement of national democracy, the document stands unrivaled in its period, and must astound those who parrot the doctrine that nationalism started with the French revolution of 1789.

The democratic nationalism of the Scots, with large numbers of independent landowners, and a robust peasantry far removed from serfdom, enabled them to survive the stormy centuries of aggression by the kings of England. Between 1377 and 1550, Scotland was at war with England for 52 years out of 174; and the King of Scots was a minor for 89 of the 182 years from 1406 to 1587. Yet in the fifteenth century, when England was riven by the Wars of the Roses, Scotland had a democratic public opinion that induced the Scots Parliament to legislate for the benefit of "the puir people that labouris the grund." Today, in the unhappily United Kingdom, Scotland still has in force no fewer than 276 of the Acts of the Scots Parliament between 1424 and 1707. Sir Archibald Alison, the leading historian of Europe in Scott's lifetime, observed: "In truth, the early precocity of Scotland in legislative wisdom, and the extraordinary provisions made by its native Parliament in remote periods, not only for the well-being of the people, but the coercion alike of regal tyranny and aristocratic oppression, and the instruction, relief and security of the poorer classes, is one of the most remarkable facts in the whole history of modern Europe."

Before 1300 the Scots intellectuals had gone to foreign universities, including Oxford, where Balliol College was mainly endowed by a Scots lady. But native universities were founded soon after 1400: St. Andrews (1412), Glasgow (1449), and King's College, Aberdeen (1494). To them the Protestants added Edinburgh (1582) and Marischal College, Aberdeen (1593). James IV had his sons tutored by Erasmus in Italy; and James V reorganized the supreme law court on an Italian model, as a Senate, or College of Justice, in 1532. Scots were at home in France under the *Auld Alliance,* and published books there before printing began at Edinburgh in 1508. The Flemish culture of the Netherlands was also influential in Scotland, in architecture, painting, and music; and much Scots trade went through Bruges or Middelburg. The Baltic area too was important, and James III and James VI married Danish princesses. From the Continent the movements for reforming the Roman church, which had become corrupt by 1500, reached Scotland, directly or through England; and the eventual form the Protestant revolution took in Scotland was a compromise between English and Continental models. The French princess Mary of Guise, widow of James V, had in the 1550's carried the Scoto-French alliance to the point where her daughter Mary Queen of Scots was married to Francis II of France, and the regnal union was accompanied by an exchange of citizenship. But the Scots lords grew restive at the presence of French garrisons, and the Scots Protestants gained support from Elizabeth Tudor of England. On the death of Mary of Guise the pro-French and Catholic party collapsed, and the Scots Parliament at Edinburgh passed an act casting off the authority of the Pope, forbidding the celebration of the Mass, and approving a Confession of Faith, drawn up by a body of ministers headed by John Knox, who had been a close colleague of John Calvin at Geneva. This parliament contained, besides earls and other magnates, over one hundred untitled landowners, lairds, sitting in person as freeholders of the Crown.

The Protestant Reformation was partly the work of landgrabbing magnates, who took and kept the lands of the Roman church, and partly that of idealists, who had read their Bibles, made available through the printing press. A Scots version not having been completed, they used the English ones, and thus English came to be the language of worship in Scotland. At a time when the national literatures of other northern nations were being strongly molded by local translations of Holy Writ, this acceptance of an English Bible by earnest Scottish readers became a strong agency for Anglicization. On the other hand the Scots rejected the Anglican model of church government by bishops appointed by the monarch, who in England had replaced the Pope as Head of the Church on earth; Scotland adopted the Presbyterian system, derived from Calvinism and the French Huguenots: kirk sessions in each parish, controlling education and poor relief; presbyteries for each group of parishes; synods for a group of presbyteries; and a national General Assembly. Calvinists abolished the distinction of clergy and laity, and believed in the priesthood of all believers and the parity of ministers. In each parish the minister, as teaching elder or preaching presbyter, had as colleagues in the kirk session a set of ruling elders, who disciplined him as well as the parishioners. They might often be lords or lairds, but the general tendency of Presbyterianism was republican and democratic. In 1581 a General Assembly perfected the organization of Scotland on Presbyterian lines, issuing a *Second Book of Discipline,* prohibiting the appointment of bishops and claiming that no king or parliament had authority to order the government of Christ's kirk or its beliefs. This had all been achieved with remarkably little fanaticism or persecution. In 1560 the Catholic church collapsed without a blow, and its adherents were pensioned off, or became converted to the Reformed ways. No Catholic was martyred until 1615, when the Episcopalians hanged the Jesuit John Ogilvie. This was after James VI had inherited the English throne in 1603, and established Episcopacy in Scotland. He adopted the slogan, "No Bishop, no king!" and many of the Scots aristocracy went along with him so far. But when his son Charles I (1625–49) tried to bribe the Scots nobles to hand over some of the old lands of the Roman church to support his Episcopal establishment, they accepted his earldoms and other titles but turned round and signed a Presbyterian manifesto, the National Covenant of 1638. This led to his farcical "Bishops' Wars" to coerce the Scots, which encouraged the English Parliament to fight him, in 1642. Things being evenly balanced, the English Parliament negotiated with the Scots Parliament a treaty, the

Solemn League and Covenant (1643), whereby the English Parliament agreed to establish Presbyterianism in England and Ireland. Then the Scots sent an army to help Oliver Cromwell win his decisive victory at Marston Moor (1644). After that the English Parliament double-crossed on its bargain. Some of the Scots negotiated with Charles I in turn, but Oliver Cromwell was by then too strong. In 1649 he had Charles I decapitated. Most of the Scots Covenanters were royalist, and the Stuart dynasty was descended, through Robert the Bruce's daughter Marjorie, from Kenneth MacAlpin and the ancient Scots dynasty from Ireland. So the Scots Parliament at once proclaimed Charles II, in exile, as king. After some delays he subscribed the two Covenants, of 1638 and 1643, and was crowned in Scotland, in 1651; but later that year his army was destroyed by Cromwell at Worcester in England. After a dictatorship, he was restored in 1660, immediately after which he re-established Episcopacy in Scotland, thinking Presbyterianism "no fit religion for a gentleman." His brother, James VII and II (1685–88), was an openly professing Roman Catholic, and persecuted the Scots Presbyterian Covenanters with hanging, branding, lopping off ears, and transportation to slavery in the West Indies and America. When his Protestant nephew and son-in-law William of Orange was invited to the throne of England in his place by a group of Whig magnates, James's party in Scotland, the Jacobites, proved a minority; and the majority of the Scots Parliament accepted William III and Mary II as rightful sovereigns, jointly. William assented to the establishment of Presbyterianism in Scotland (1690), though he favored Anglican Episcopacy in England and Ireland. His successor, Queen Anne (1702–14), not having children capable of surviving, the problem of the royal succession engaged the two parliaments of Scotland and England. A personal union of the two kingdoms, under the antiquarian style "Great Britain," had proved workable since 1603 with good will on both sides, and tact by the monarch; and in recent times the dominions of Canada, New Zealand, and the rest have found it workable to acknowledge the British Crown while retaining sovereign self-government in their own affairs. But in the early 1700's many English thought that a separate Scots parliament was bound to be a source for French intrigue; and many Scots became willing to sacrifice their native parliament to secure the Protestant succession, and to gain admittance to the English colonies overseas. Proposals for a federal union being rejected by the English, a treaty was made, with effect from May 1, 1707, uniting the two parliaments and establishing a new Parliament of the United Kingdom, in which Scotland was to be represented by forty-five Members in the House of Commons and sixteen representative peers in the House of Lords. The main motives were religious and commercial. It was an anti-Papist alliance, and an insular and colonial common market. The Scots Presbyterian church and Scots law, with the Scots law courts, were preserved, as were the self-governing powers of the Scots burghs.

In the Scots Parliament, a single-chamber legislature of three Estates, the lords voted for the Treaty of Union by 42 to 19, the Commissioners for Shires (lairds) by 38 to 30, and the Commissioners for Burghs (burgesses) by 30 to 20: in all 110 for and 69 against. But public feeling in the country was much more strongly hostile to it. The Jacobite party sought to exploit dissatisfaction by a series of risings, notably in 1715 and 1745; but the Scots majority had no desire to expel the Protestant family of Hanover, who had come to the throne in 1714, for Catholic claimants backed by the despotic kings of France. Though some families and clans, notably north of the Tay, were Jacobite, through old loyalties and hatreds, even when Prince Charles Edward held court at Edinburgh in 1745, the Jacobite Lord Elcho testifies that "not one of the mob who were so fond of seeing him ever ask'd to enlist in his service." The Jacobite faction was far from being a national party; there was in the eighteenth century no national party; but there were abundant manifestations of national feeling, largely focused on Edinburgh, which remained a national capital as headquarters of the Scottish law and church, and seat of a north British sub-government. Such was the historical background for Sir Walter Scott.

2

The Economic and Political Background

SEVENTEEN CENTURIES OF HISTORY had given the eighteenth-century Scots a tradition of unconquered independence, with an ancient monarchy of Celtic origin, distinctive legal and religious institutions, a numerous and mainly poor aristocracy, a hardy peasantry wth a zeal for education fostered by the church, and a multi-centered cultural activity in different languages—Gaelic, Latin, Scots, and English. There was also a vigorous tradition of individual careerism, in France under the *Auld Alliance*, in the Netherlands, the Germanies, Sweden, Russia, and, since 1603, England. But the religious convulsions of the seventeenth century had left the country's economy much more backward relatively than it had been before the king and his courtiers moved to London in 1603. After 1707, with the end of the religious wars, Scots landowners gave more attention to improving their estates; and an agricultural revolution led to a growth of wealth, which enabled more of them to spend more time in Edinburgh, which thus became, from about 1760, a boom town, an international center for tourism and enlightenment, the setting for a Golden Age in which the elite culture of the upper classes was increasingly diffused to the whole people.

The peculiar social structure of Edinburgh appears from the first census after Scott's death. With its seaport of Leith, Edinburgh contained, in 1841, 163,726 persons, of whom 7,463 were "bankers, professional men, or capitalists." They outnumbered the 4,446 laborers and the 792 employed in manufactures. There were 19,764 persons engaged in trades and retail business; 1,422 male servants and 12,429 female servants; and a "remainder of males of various kinds," totaling 4,113. Most of the professional men were lawyers. For them, and the medical men, bankers, and *rentiers*, the main source of wealth was the boom in land values.

On 20,000,000 acres of land Scotland had in 1707 little over 1,000,000 persons. There were over sixty towns, but all small. Even Edinburgh then had only 30,000 inhabitants. The landowners had been interested mainly in having numerous tenants ready to supply men-at-arms in troubled times; but from about 1690 minds began to turn to securing the maximum money income from estates. Scots lawyers had been going to the Dutch universities of Leiden and Utrecht, where they learned, besides Roman law, Dutch ideas of drainage and cultivation. It was usual for Scots landed families to train younger sons for law, medicine, the church, or commerce. Thus David Hume, younger son of the Laird of Ninewells, a cadet of the family holding the earldom of Home, had an uncle who was minister of the family parish, Chirnside; one cousin became minister in turn, and another a baker in Edinburgh. There were 154 Scots peerage titles on the Union Roll of 1707, of which only 2 were held by families raised from trading (Napier and Hope). There were also hundreds of lairds, reckoned noble by Scots heraldic usage and by that of France, as Louis XIV's great minister Colbert found useful, when he secured noble status by proof of descent from burgesses of Inverness who held a near-by barony as lairds of Castlehill. It is a feature of the eighteenth century that lawyers, doctors, ministers, and merchants used their knowledge and skills to promote the landed families to which they were connected. Edinburgh was the winter headquarters of the landed class, and the center of diffusion of modern ideas to every parish in the land, in land reclamation, architecture, and industry.

The Presbyterians were keen to spread education in every parish, and to promote any talented youth who might develop into a good preacher of the Word. If he failed to secure a kirk, he could become a schoolmaster, or a clerk to a lawyer or banker or merchant. Scotland soon produced an exportable surplus of competent managers of various types of business. One can hardly exaggerate the practical interest taken by the upper classes, including literary men, in land improvement and unified resource development. Walter Scott planted thousands of trees with his own hands, as did a Duke of Atholl. Judges would inspect samples of turnip seed, and compare notes on types of plow, in the intervals of murder trials. Parish ministers were practical farmers, and knowledgeable about local industry. To them we owe the *Statistical Accounts* of 1793 and 1845.

Edinburgh lawyers took the lead in better farming, by land enclosure; granting of long leases to efficient tenants; draining, liming, and applying marl to land; planting trees for shelter and timber; sowing clover and rye grass, and turnips for winter feed for cattle, a main item of Scots export trade. Societies of improvers gave premiums for new machines. Thus James Small invented a "swing" plow in 1764, operable by one man with two horses, replacing the massive old plow needing three men and ten or more oxen. Andrew Meikle's threshing machine (1786) did away with many man-hours of flail-wielding. Problems of redundancy of labor were mitigated partly by employing more men in draining, building, and improving roads and canals, or in cottage industries using flax, hemp, and wool as raw materials. But many thousands of Scots were recruited into regiments raised by the London government, or emigrated to England and overseas.

The financing of improvements was carried out by independent Scottish banks: the Bank of Scotland (1695), the Royal Bank of Scotland (1727), and the British Linen Bank, set up in 1746 to promote imports of flax, for sale to spinners, and purchases of spun yarns for sale to weavers. The latter also organized bleachfields and warehouses, and, in the bygoing, issued its own notes, thus becoming a banker. From 1763 it dropped its other activities and emerged as an important bank, using its local agencies as branches. Glasgow developed two banks of its own in 1750, but Edinburgh remained the financial center of Scotland. It is argued that the Scots Law of society, or company formation, was more conducive to enterprise than the common law of England, and that the

Presbyterian superintendence of morals by kirk sessions made it easier for agents of a bank to obtain an evaluation of the character of an applicant for a loan. In the financial crisis of 1825, London interests attempted to remove by statute the independent credit-issuing powers of the Scottish banks, but were frustrated by a national resistance, to which Scott contributed his *Letters of Malachi Malagrowther*. In merchant banking the most notable house was that of John Coutts and Company, founded in 1723 in a small Edinburgh apartment. The savings bank movement grew rapidly in Scotland from a start in 1810 by the parish minister of Ruthwell, Dumfriesshire, Dr. Henry Duncan.

In 1727 the London Parliament set up a Board of Trustees for Manufactures, to disburse some of the money promised to Scotland in 1707 for undertaking a share in the relatively large national debt of England. It did some good, for the linen industry and the herring fisheries, in particular. But the government of Walpole simultaneously became unpopular by taxing malt. This led to riots, and the shooting of Glasgow citizens by English soldiers. Taxes on French claret and brandy, for long favored Scots drinks, turned smuggling into a national pastime. An uncle of the poet Burns, Samuel Broun, was censured from the pulpit of Kirkoswald, not for smuggling simply but for smuggling on the Sabbath. Direct government control, for good or ill, hardly existed in the early decades of the parliamentary union. Landowners got ahead with their improvements, and politics were managed mainly by two great noblemen, the second and third Dukes of Argyll, until 1761, when the third Duke died, leaving his family's influence to his cousin, John Stuart, third Earl of Bute, who in 1762 became the first of that curious line of Scots Prime Ministers of Great Britain which includes Aberdeen, Gladstone, Rosebery, Balfour, Campbell-Bannerman, Bonar Law, Ramsay Macdonald, Harold Macmillan, and Sir Alec Douglas-Home.

Bute came into politics by accident. One day in 1747 rain stopped play at an English cricket match, and Bute was summoned by Frederick Prince of Wales to make a fourth at whist. The handsome Scots peer took the fancy of the Princess of Wales, Augusta of Saxe-Coburg, mother of the future George III, to whom, as a mentally retarded youth, Bute became a sort of father-figure. Soon after coming to the throne, George III was trying to wind up the Seven Years' War, and made Bute premier in May, 1762, to do so. It was in Bute's premiership that Scots careerists first made a major breakthrough into public positions of power and profit in the growing British Empire. By favoring Scots, Bute disobliged a noted demagogue of the day, John Wilkes, who, with the satirist Charles Churchill, carried on a brisk journalistic war of anti-Scotticism in *The North Briton,* against the Scots novelist Tobias Smollett, who wrote for the government organ, *The Briton.* Bute, as Chancellor of Marischal College, Aberdeen, had patronized James Macpherson's purported translation of the ancient Celtic epic, *Fingal*; in discussions of its authenticity political animus inflamed literary and historical skepticism. The success of the Ossianic material in sweeping over Europe was, in part, a *succès de scandale.* Its influence affected minds so diverse as Goethe and Napoleon.

23

The patriotic fervor of the Scots was provoked, all the more so that Scots regiments had been doing more than their fair share in the conquest of empire in Canada and India.

Warfare as a trade had been practiced by the Scots for centuries. Under the *Auld Alliance* with France, they had become Constables and Marshals and Dukes, and furnished a royal bodyguard. When Napoleon I invaded Russia, he had a Scots Marshal Macdonald, while the Russian Emperor had a commander of Aberdeenshire origin, Prince Barclay de Tolly. Frederick the Great's favorite commader was the Scots Marshal Keith. Hundreds of thousands of lower rank Scots had fought as galloglasses in the quarrels of Anglo-Irish chiefs, mercenaries in the Thirty Years' War, on both sides, or as a Scots Brigade in the Netherlands. The London politicians, after some qualms about the danger of Jacobite sentiments, began to exploit Scotland systematically as a source of man power. At the same time they transferred contracts for the supply of arms, uniforms, and so forth, from Scottish manufacturers to English, who were, of course, paid in part by Scottish taxes—one aspect of the siphoning off of wealth to London and its neighborhood, which made Scotland, in the phrase of Lord Rosebery, one of the Scots prime ministers, "the milch-cow of the Empire." Some Independent Companies, raised in 1725 for policing the Highlands against Jacobites, were in 1739 embodied into the regiment famed as "The Black Watch," garbed in kilts of a dark tartan not distinctive of any clan. After the 1745 Rising the London government banned the tartan, distrusting even the clans that had fought for it; and abolished the feudal jurisdictions of lords and lairds that had enabled them to levy their tenants for the Jacobite cause. In the war of 1756–63, when a militia was raised in England for local defense against a possible French landing, the Scots were not trusted with one. Some Englishmen, however, favored enlisting Scots. James Wolfe, the conqueror of Quebec, wrote: "I should imagine that Highlanders might be of use. They are hardy, intrepid, accustomed to a rough country, and no great mischief if they fall. How can you better employ a secret enemy than by making his end conducive to the common good? If this sentiment should take wind what an execrable and bloody being should I be considered?" The elder Pitt, Lord Chatham, backed Wolfe, telling Parliament: "I looked for Valour, and found it in the North." The Highlanders so recruited were treated, like Uriah the Hittite, as expendable. The *Edinburgh Courant* newspaper protested, on July 18, 1763: "Were not Highlanders put upon every enterprise where nothing was to be gotten but broken bones?" Sir Thomas Innes of Learney, Lord Lyon King of Arms, wrote: "The British Empire is really the creation of the Scots, for, prior to the Union, England could not even retain the territories which it from time to time inherited. . . . Whenever a war breaks out, the War Office is thoughtful to exploit the Clan Spirit." Mr. Duncan Duff, in a detailed study, *Scotland's War Losses*, remarked: "To enlist the Scots voluntarily every sentiment, feudal, clan, or local, that could be exploited, was utilised. . . . Scots soldiers had to feel that they were fighting in some measure for Scotland, with fellow-countrymen as comrades in Scottish formations, with national distinctions in designation and uniform. . . . How were the ranks filled? In some districts tradition asserts that recruits were kidnapped. Assurance of security to parents in the tenure of their holdings, payment of generous bounties by noblemen commissioned to raise regiments, promise of preferment in the occupancy of farms by relatives or by the soldiers on their return, a crude conscription under which those charged with petty offences were given the alternative of prosecution or enlistment: all were inducements."

In Scott's time, Mr. Duff remarked: "Scots were fighting in India . . . in far greater numbers than the ratio of their population to that of the United Kingdom—one ninth—justified." The same obtained in other theaters of war. At Aboukir, Scots battalions were 30 per cent of those engaged, at Alexandria 31 per cent, at the Cape of Good Hope 42 per cent, while at Waterloo eight Scottish battalions fought in a battle where the total British infantry strength was thirty-one. Of the four regiments singled out by the Duke of Wellington for special commendation, three were Scots.

At the conclusion of campaigns survivors often were not brought back to Scotland. Many were encouraged by grants of land to settle in British North America, a territory which has, to be sure, a good deal to be said for it, even if it is not Scotland. Further emigrants often went to join time-expired soldiers who had colonized the transatlantic territories; and some of the Highland proprietors forcibly cleared people off their lands to make way for Lowland tenants offering rents for sheepwalks. Later, in the middle nineteenth century, many of the sheepwalks were turned into deer forests, with the result that a huge tract of the north of Scotland became a wilderness devoted to sport. The same processes produced similar results in the Borders and southern uplands of Scotland.

The net effect of these contributions of Scots man power to the United Kingdom forces was, on the human side, a massive depopulation of hundreds of rural parishes; but on the credit side one may place the growth of Scots influence in the English-speaking world at large, especially in North America. Further, some fresh capital investment and technical know-how accrued from officers who had survived with sizable fortunes. Merchants, too, increasingly took global views. East coast ports had declined after the Union, but the Clyde ports of Glasgow and Greenock began to develop a trade from the American colonies and the West Indies, notably in the tobacco of Virginia and Carolina, which was much in demand, to smoke, chew, or sniff up in the form of snuff powder. Glasgow merchants began to compete seriously with those of Bristol and London in transatlantic trade, and a series of speculative fortunes helped the investment in land reclamation, and new industries, for example the coachbuilding of Edinburgh. In 1783 an Edinburgh coachmaker sold 1,000 crane-necked carriages to Paris. Lord Provost Creech claimed that "Coaches and chaises were constructed as elegantly in Edinburgh as anywhere in Europe, and, it may be added, stronger and cheaper." Many were exported from Leith to St. Petersburg and the Baltic area. In 1759 an act of parliament was obtained for enlarging the navigable channel of the Clyde, after which Glasgow became a boom town. The same year saw the start of the Carron ironworks, in which the Englishmen Roebuck and Garbett joined a Scot, William Cadell, near the Firth of Forth. This enterprise began to get contracts for naval guns, including eventually many of those that won the battle of Trafalgar (1805). As Scots influence grew in the London government Scottish makers of ropes and canvas began also to receive Admiralty contracts. The intermingling of politics and economics was manifested in the career of Henry Dundas, first Viscount Melville (1742–1811), a member of a famous family of lawyers in Edinburgh, with well-improved estates near by. He allied himself with the younger Pitt, prime minister from 1783 to 1801 and 1804 to 1806, and became treasurer of the Navy, president of the Board of Control for India, minister of war, and political manager for Scotland. Of the 45 Commons seats, 30 were for county constituencies, which had, in 1788, only 2,624 qualified electors, many of them dependent on some great landowner. Edinburgh returned an M.P. by itself, but the other burghs were grouped into fourteen constituencies, again with relatively few voters in each. The party managers knew, within a narrow margin, what inducement would win the vote of most electors: for example, a commission in the army or the navy, a clerkship of the East India Company, a place in the customs or excise, for a son or a son-in-law or a nephew, or a wife's first cousin twice removed. For the Scots were very clannish.

"Harry" Dundas was an amiable, "folksy" character, who commonly spoke the broadest of Scotch in Pitt's Cabinet, and liked to roister in a lowly Scottish drinking shop, as did many of his fashionable contemporaries, like the Duke of Buccleugh, though each had his country palace to retire to after his "pub crawl." Dundas managed the restoration, in 1784, of Jacobite estates forfeited after the 1745 Rising; and in 1782 the legal suppression of the Highland dress was ended. In 1805 the House of Commons censured him, by the Speaker's casting vote, for misapplying public funds while Treasurer of the navy, but next year, on his impeachment, after a fifteen-day trial the House of Lords acquitted him of every charge. He seems to have been guilty of negligence, not of fraud. In 1821 he was posthumously honored by a Doric column 136 feet high, with a 14-foot statue on top, costing about £6,000, mainly subscribed by "gentlemen connected with the Navy."

Clannish political management, and lucrative jobbery, were pursued by some Scots in America also, as elucidated by Ian C. C. Graham, in his book *Colonists from Scotland*. He writes: "The conservatism of the great majority of the Scots in the colonies, coupled with the envy inspired by their commercial success and political power, exposed them to mounting unpopularity and abuse from Americans." But American aspirations also had significant Scottish support, notably from the poet Burns. David Hume, who was host to Benjamin Franklin in Edinburgh, wrote in 1775: "I am an American in my Principles, and wish we woud let them alone to govern or misgovern themselves as they think proper." Two Scots signed the Declaration of Independence, including James Wilson, later a Justice of the Supreme Court, and a main framer of the United States Constitution. He was farseeing, and most of the proposals of his that were rejected initially were adopted by later amendments. Even if upper-class Scots might be Tory, there were plenty of others, notably those connected with Ulster. President Theodore Roosevelt, himself part-Scots, testified to the pioneering leadership of "that stern and virile people, the Scotch-Irish. They . . . became the vanguard of our civilization. . . . These were the men who first declared for American independence. . . . For generations their whole ecclesiastical and scholastic systems had been found fundamentally democratic." Perhaps the oddest character was John Paul Jones, the Scot who is claimed as founder of the American Navy. Some find it odd that Flora Macdonald, who in 1746 helped save "Bonnie Prince Charlie" after Culloden, was loyal to the Hanoverians in 1777, and emigrated from North Carolina rather than take an oath of allegiance to the American patriot government. By that time not only the dominant elements in Scottish society but the majority of the people were reconciled to the union with England, in principle even if not in detail. An economic and social symbiosis had developed, with a hybrid Anglo-Scottish culture, focused on the double city of Edinburgh then developing.

3

The Two Edinburghs

THE OLD EDINBURGH of the Middle Ages grew; the New Edinburgh of Scott's age was planned, to produce an example of urban living hardly rivaled anywhere. The need to plan arose from noisome overcrowding, and the means to finance the new residential town came from the profits of the landowners' revolution.

A volcanic rock 443 feet above sea level, with almost perpendicular west and south faces, was used for a castle by Welsh and Pictish kings before the Scots placed their chief archives there. Bruce razed it, all but the chapel of St. Margaret, but his son David II refortified it and the Stewarts embellished it. It housed the old regalia of the Scots dynasty, hidden from 1707 until 1818, when Scott had them brought out, to become a tourist attraction. In his day it could hold a garrison of 2,000 men, and its esplanade was a favorite promenade, with superb views south, beyond the Pentland hills, and north, beyond the valley of gardens and the New Town to the estuary of the Forth and the hills of Fife and beyond.

From the castle a ridge sloped gently eastward a mile, down to the abbey of Holyrood (1128) where stood the palace of the Stewarts, as rebuilt for Charles II, with sheep grazing in the courtyards, and cesspools and dung-heaps all round, but some suites of rooms inside maintained by the Duke of Hamilton and the Earls of Lauderdale, Breadalbane, and Selkirk, where they housed dowagers and minor fashionable relatives. The future Charles X of France, in exile, lived there from 1796 to 1802 and enjoyed the debtors' sanctuary rights, for which others paid two guineas a year to the Bailie of the Hereditary Keeper. They were free from arrest in and near Holyrood, and on the King's Park, including the minor mountain Arthur Seat (820 feet), and the precipitous Salisbury Crags, David Hume's favorite walk. The French prince kept a mistress in the park.

From castle down to palace ran the Royal Mile, broad enough for five coaches abreast, between buildings of stone, with slated or tiled roofs, with twelve or even sixteen stories. It looked like a canyon with windows, and had the effect on eighteenth-century visitors now felt by a rustic among Manhattan's skyscrapers. Tall chimneys belched smoke from coal, burned at the rate of about 500 tons a day, in the 1790's costing half a guinea for 23 hundredweight. The nickname of the city was "*Auld Reekie*" ("Old Smoky"). But coal smoke was less offensive than the pervasive odor of human excreta from the tall overcrowded buildings. At 10:00 P.M. drums gave warning, after which the day's slops were thrown onto the streets, with the cry "*Gardyloo*" (from French, "*Prenez garde à l'eau*"). These so-called *flouers o'*

Embro lay until 7:00 A.M., when scavengers collected them to sell. But there was no collection on Sunday, and no water carriers worked that day either. In spite of near success in the 1770's and 1780's Old Edinburgh never really beat its problems of sewage disposal and water supply; but people got used to them, like the courtiers of Versailles with its countless *chaises percées*. An odd feature of the Edinburgh scene was the *Wha wants me?* man, who perambulated the main thoroughfare carrying a *chaise percée*, and wearing an outsize cloak, to give privacy to the user of his itinerant convenience. There was much of the farmyard about the old city, with pigs running in the streets, as at Paris, kestrels nesting on the Castle rock, corncrakes sounding in the meadows, and kingfishers darting along the Water of Leith where the mills ground the city's grain. To keep within the medieval wall the citizens had built intensively on their strips of land, and in each tenement, or apartment block, called a "land," there would be several families living in flats, having access by a common stair. The lower classes lived on the lowest and highest floors, with countesses, judges, lairds, and merchants in the middle, as in old Paris; and the classes appear to have mingled with great amity. There was much elegance, as in the house of the ancestors of the Prime Minister Gladstone in the Lawnmarket, with its arcade on the street level, where passers-by could shelter from rain and view the textiles available from the merchant, and its painted ceilings for handsome rooms upstairs. Many houses had decorative moldings with painted and gilded coats of arms and pious mottoes. Exterior walls were painted in white or pale colors. Even the

Gothic, partly Norman, church of St. Giles was whitewashed to the level of its knot of flying buttresses, forming an imperial crown to represent Scotland's sovereignty.

Residential segregation began to develop in 1727, with the building of James's Court, an exclusive block where Hume once lived and Boswell was host to Dr. Johnson. In 1755 the population was 57,220; in 1801, when Scott was aged thirty, 82,560; and in 1831 nearly double that, 162,403. Scott lived in a booming, expanding town all his life. In 1751 there were only 6,845 houses; at the first census after Scott's death there were 22,523. In 1753 there were only 12 streets, and 22 wynds (through lanes), as against 8 courts and 260 closes (very small courtyards). Where coaches could not reach, sedan chairs plied, carried mainly by Gaelic-speaking Highlanders.

The first expansion was to the south, notably with George's Square (1766), 660 by 500 feet, to which Scott's lawyer father moved, near a park, the Meadows, formed after draining the Burgh Loch. That was a private speculation, but public enterprise was also being promoted, notably by Lord Provost George Drummond, from 1724. Chiefly to him was due the new Royal Infirmary (1738), by William Adam, father of more famous sons; and the Royal Exchange (1753), with its arcaded Corinthian courtyard. The merchants preferred to do business in the open air, and it was turned over to become Council Chambers (1811). In 1766 the Town Council held a competition for the plan of a New Town, won by James Craig, the young nephew of the best-selling poet James Thomson. This was laid out on a gentle ridge running west to east, parallel with the Royal Mile, across a valley, at that

34

time filled with the shallow North Loch. When the North Bridge over the valley was finished (1772), rich men began to build houses in the New Town, costing about £2,000 each. David Hume was one, and the street beside it was jocularly named for him, St. David's. The New Town was further joined to the Old by a grandiose Mound, begun in 1783, of earth dug from foundations. Creech, Burns's publisher, calls it "a work unrivalled by any but Alexander the Great's at Tyre," and reckons that it contained 1,305,750 cartloads of earth.

Craig laid out a main street, George Street, along the ridge, and formed two terrace streets, Princes Street and Queen Street, to be the southern and northern limits of the scheme. In between them and George Street he formed parallel interior streets, Rose Street and Thistle Street, called for the national flowers of the neighboring nations. The Town Council ruled that each house in the three major streets should have a height of 48 feet from basement to wall-head, and that none should be of more than three floors, exclusive of a basement and an attic. The houses had to be aligned behind the sunken area separating the basement from the street. Care was taken that the end houses of each block should be of adequate width for the good appearance of the street. Elsewhere builders could please themselves. Commonly, houses had three windows in breadth, and accommodation on five floors, served by internal stairways. The material was mainly a handsome yellowish-grey sandstone. As the buildings proceeded westward, more use was made of porches and pillars, pediments, sculptured moldings, and ironwork balconies. At the east end of George Street was St. Andrew's Square, and at the west Charlotte Square, on the north side of which Robert Adam's block had a single palatial façade (1791). In later extensions of the New Town to north and west it became regular to treat each block as a unity, and some delightful effects were produced with crescents, circuses, and even an octagon. Craig had planned that George Street should have its vistas to east and west terminated by great churches of St. Andrew and St. George. But the space for St. Andrew's Church had been usurped by Sir Laurence Dundas for a mansion built by Sir William Chambers, and the St. Andrew's Church had to be put on the north side of George Street (1785). Its design, by an engineer officer, Major Frazer, was the result of a competition. Its steeple, added by William Sibbald, housed a set of eight bells, rung in the English style. This is an example of the growing Anglo-Scottish syncretism of the times, for thitherto the Scots had followed Continental fashions in bell-ringing. The great west church, St. George's, with a dome 150 feet high, was by Robert Reid (1814). The finest building of the New Town was Robert Adam's Register House (1774), for the national archives. It closes the north vista down the North Bridge from the Old Town. Behind it lay a rough hill, Bunker's Hill, and east of that the road to Leith, and a ravine below the Calton Hill, which rises to 356 feet above sea level. This was an age of philhellenism, and people early compared the Calton to the Athenian Acropolis. About 1814 a fashion arose of calling Edinburgh "The Modern Athens," and some of the buildings put on the Calton were of Hellenic inspiration. The Earl of Elgin, a Scot, rescued from the Turks some of the finest sculptures of ancient Greece, and this partly influenced the Highland Society of Scotland, in 1816, to launch a scheme for a National Monument, to commemorate the Scots slain at Waterloo, which was to start with a replica of the Parthenon at Athens. On George IV's visit in 1822, the Duke of Hamilton, as Grand Master Mason of Scotland, was commissioned to lay the foundation, and twelve splendid Doric columns were erected. Funds and enthusiasm then ran out; and the inchoate temple still stands unfinished, symbolizing nobody knows what. The Calton Hill was embellished too with a new Royal High School, inspired by the "Theseum" (or Hephaistieion) at Athens; monuments to Burns and the philosopher Dugald Stewart, partly inspired by the choragic monument of Lysicrates; and, among other edifices, a much-battlemented baronial prison, since mainly demolished. Mr. Ian Lindsay, in *Georgian Edinburgh*, remarks: "Its place has been taken by a large modern structure of international design through which London transmits its instructions to the Scottish Nation."

In building new churches, Hellenism on the whole prevailed, but there were several Gothic experiments, not only among the Episcopalians and Roman Catholics, from both of whom the legal disabilities were removed in the 1790's, when fear of Jacobitism was replaced by detestation of French revolutionary extremism. Scott, though bred a Presbyterian, joined his Episcopalian wife in worshiping in the new St. George's Episcopal Chapel, York Place. He kept Christmas, while his old mother confined her observance to giving New Year's gifts.

Not much commerce intruded at first into the New Town. The boom area for shops was in a southward extension from the Old Town, where a South Bridge was built, in the 1780's, on the line of the North Bridge. Prices were paid as high as £150,000 an acre, the highest in Europe. Here in 1789 the foundation was laid for a new building for the University, with Doric monolith columns 26 feet high; but it was too ambitious for the funds available. Besides regular squares and streets, the outskirts of Edinburgh were embellished with many elegant villas in walled parks. Most streets had gardens or parks attached which were managed jointly on behalf of the houseowners; but the painter Raeburn, in laying out Ann Street, attached individual gardens to each house.

Edinburgh had no strong array of industries: a few breweries; tanneries; paper mills; coachbuilding works; establishments for the manufacture of shawls, cashmeres, buttons, umbrellas, and starch for hair powder; and printing shops. Leith in 1791 had 5 master shipbuilders, employing 152 carpenters, at about 1 shilling 10 pence daily. It was building ships of about 300 tons, and there were some hundreds of them sailing to the Baltic. In 1793 there were two stage coaches daily to London, taking usually four days; but by 1820 a steamboat could go there from Leith in sixty hours. It is curious that, when Scott was ten years old, Leith had to be fortified with a battery of nine guns to fend off John Paul

Jones, operating near by with three armed vessels and terrifying the coast.

By 1790, Edinburgh had 1,427 four-wheeled carriages and 462 two-wheeled, besides 6,450 wains and carts. There were a great number of hackney coaches for hire, with excellent horses. There was a great boom in retail trade for fashionable appurtenances. Creech found that, in 1783 already, nearly the most common profession in town was that of "haberdasher," in which category he included mercer, milliner, linen draper, hatter, hosier and glover. He adds that perfumers had splendid shops in every principal street. Some of them kept bears, to kill for greasing ladies' and gentlemen's, hair. The hairdressers' busiest day was Sunday.

The segregation of the upper classes in the New Town caused a rapid decline in the standards of the Old Town. Scott wrote to Lady Anne Lindsay, author of the affecting ballad "Auld Robin Gray," about her mother, the Countess of Balcarres, a neighbor of his uncle in an old apartment block; he recalls the Indian screen and the harpsichord, and goes on: "I suppose the close, once too clean to soil the hem of your ladyship's garment, is now a resort for the lowest mechanics. . . . It is, to be sure, more picturesque to lament the desolation of towers on hills and haughs, than the degradation of an Edinburgh close; but I cannot help thinking on the simple and cosie retreats where worth and talent, and elegance to boot, were often nestled, and which now are the resort of misery, filth, poverty, and vice."

In earlier times Scots divisions were vertical, based on locality and clan; now in Edinburgh horizontal social tensions arose, sharpened by the division between New Town and Old. But this was not the only dichotomy in the life of the Anglo-Scottish double city.

4

Religion, Law, and Philosophy

SEPARATION OF CHURCH AND STATE was an almost completely accomplished fact in the Scotland of Hume and Scott. The General Assembly of the Church of Scotland claimed to be a legislature and a law court wholly independent, in its own spheres of government, of the King of Great Britain and the United Kingdom Parliament and the London government. An *Act for Securing the Protestant Religion and Presbyterian Church Government* formed part of the international treaty of 1707. On accession, each British monarch was to take an oath that he would "inviolably maintain and preserve the foresaid settlement of the True Protestant Religion, with the Government, Worship, Discipline, Right and Priviledges of this Church, as above established by the Laws of this Kingdom." This is still the position, as restated in "Articles Declaratory" passed by the General Assembly of 1921, which assert: "This Church, as part of the Universal Church wherein the Lord Jesus Christ has appointed a government in the hands of Church office-bearers, receives from Him, its Divine

King and head, and from Him alone, the right and power, subject to no civil authority, to legislate and to adjudicate finally, in all matters of doctrine, worship, government and discipline in the Church. . . .

"This Church acknowledges the divine appointment and authority of the civil magistrate within his own sphere. . . . The Church and the State owe mutual duties to each other, and acting within their respective spheres may signally promote each other's welfare." The basic principle was stated in personal terms when Andrew Melville, as a commissioner of the General Assembly in 1596, gripping King James VI by the sleeve, called him "God's sillie vassal" ("simple dependent") and declared: "There are two kings and two kingdoms in Scotland. There is Christ Jesus the King and His kingdom the Kirk, whose subject King James the Sixth is, and of whose Kingdom not a king, nor a lord, nor a head, but a member." William of Orange had accepted this principle in 1690, and so did the House of Hanover from 1714. But a large number of the Scottish lords and lairds never at heart accepted it; and their nonacceptance greatly colored the ways in which institutional religion worked in the eighteenth century.

In the Presbyterian system, established by statute and by international treaty, the General Assembly, meeting annually in Edinburgh in May, was the chief law court in a hierarchy of courts, and the chief legislature. The lowest court and council was the kirk session in each parish, consisting of the minister and elders. These elders were not deacons, as in the Episcopal church, but presbyters, having spiritual and

42

ruling authority in the church in no way inferior to that of ministers. The parish minister was simply "the preaching Elder." In John Knox's *First Book of Discipline* (1560) it had been laid down that ministers should be tested, approved, and inducted by other ministers and elders. By Hume's time the presbytery did the licensing of candidates for the ministry. There were more than nine hundred parishes in Scotland, grouped into over sixty presbyteries, constituted by the parish minister and one elder from each parish. The presbyteries in turn were grouped into twelve synods. Presbyteries exercised, in their sphere, some of the powers of bishops in Episcopalian churches; and synods, some of those of archbishops. The annual General Assembly was made up of the parish minister and one elder from about one-fourth of the parishes in the country, which were represented in rotation. Each body, from presbytery to Assembly, chose its moderator, a mere chairman. Each minister chaired his own kirk session. A minister or elder had the right of nomination to the eldership, and acceptance of his nominee lay with the communicant heads of families in the congregation. A crucial problem was that of the right to nominate, or present, candidates for the ministry of a parish. Some parish churches had been founded originally by members of a particular landowning family; and their successors after the Reformation were allowed, as patrons, to present candidates; but such candidates had to be tested and licensed by presbyteries, even in periods when the later Stuarts had imposed bishops; and a candidate, after due licensing, still had to receive a "call" from the elders and heritors, that is, owners of real estate in the parish, who might not be elders. Payment of the minister's stipend and upkeep of his manse, or official residence, was a statutory burden of the landowners, who had to pay teind, one-tenth of the produce of the soil and of all natural increase, in cereals, livestock, cheese, eggs, wool, and the rest. This levy became a fixed charge, and could be commuted for a capital payment.

It had long been common for landowners to use patronage to provide for younger sons or relatives. Thus one of David Hume's uncles became minister of the local parish, Chirnside. But many lairds were Episcopalians and Jacobites, and it was natural for the Presbyterian party in 1690 to abolish the rights of patrons. The Act for Security in theory safeguarded that position after the Union; but the Tory ministry in London, in Queen Anne's reign, lost no time in breaking it. The Presbyterians thought, after 1690 and 1707, that they had a legal monopoly of institutional religion in Scotland, but in fact they could not suppress the influential minority of Episcopalians. In 1709 an Episcopal pastor, the Rev. James Greenshields, began holding services in Edinburgh, using the Anglican prayer book. The presbytery deprived him of his ministerial office, and the magistrates put him in prison. The Court of Session rejected his appeal, and he then appealed to the House of Lords, which sustained his appeal and made the magistrates pay his costs (1711). This raises the point that the Covenants of the seventeenth century had been concerned with purity of religion, not with liberty of conscience, or tolerance for dissenters from the orthodoxy arrived at by the "common sense" of the majority. When Boswell took Dr.

Johnson to see "the English chapel" at Montrose, he reminded him "that episcopals were but *dissenters* here; they
were only *tolerated*. 'Sir, (said he,) we are here, as Christians
in Turkey.'"

Following up the House of Lords decision, the United
Kingdom Parliament in 1712 passed a Toleration Act, sanc-
tioning Episcopalian worship in Scotland, contrary to the
terms of the Treaty, and imposing on all ministers the obligation to take an oath of allegiance to the reigning monarch,
who, by English law, must belong to the Church of England,
and was in theory head of it. Extremist Presbyterians refused the oath, and so did Episcopalians adhering to the
exiled "Old Pretender." Also in 1712, Parliament passed a
Patronage Act, asserting the right of individual lay patrons
to appoint ministers, and excluding the right of elders and
heritors conferred by the Scots statute of 1690. This act was
unconstitutional, and led to several splits in the Church of
Scotland, and eventually to the great Disruption of 1843. At
first there were merely annual Assembly protests against patronage: then, in 1733, Ebenezer Erskine and three other ministers formally seceded from their "uncovenanted" brethren,
and formed the Associate Presbytery. As other ministers and
congregations joined this Original Secession, the church deposed them all (1740). In formulating its position, the Associate Presbytery denounced the failure to renew the Covenants,
the toleration of "Episcopal hirelings," the uncovenanted
Union with England, Christmas holidays in the law courts,
the yoke of patronage, the toleration of assemblies for danc-
ing, and even the repeal of statutes against witchcraft.

The Seceders suffered a split of their own in 1747, a minority being unwilling to approve an oath, required to be taken by new burgesses in certain burghs, to uphold "the true Protestant religion presently professed within this realm." For them that meant the Established church, which they had all been busy denouncing. These Anti-Burghers marched out, and in 1748 formed the General Associate Synod, which forthrightly denounced and deposed from the ministry their recent colleagues in the Associate Presbytery. Sects began to multiply. For instance, the *Auld Lichts* (adherents of the "old light") maintained that the civil power should have a duty to impose Seceder orthodoxy upon everyone. Anti-Lifters forbade ministers to lift up the bread and wine of communion during consecration of them. Scotland also was visited by Evangelists from outside, notably George Whitefield, a leading English Methodist, in 1741. And there were various evangelical stirrings inside the *Auld Kirk,* the Establishment, itself. In Lanarkshire, in 1742, the Rev. William McCulloch, minister of Cambuslang, organized a mass communion of thirty thousand persons, with extravagant manifestations of repentance by sinners and joy by those who felt themselves in a state of grace. For most of the century from 1740 the evangelical movements remained inside the Establishment, and every Assembly saw symptoms of a struggle for power with the Moderates, which involved David Hume's philosophy, as well as such literary matters as the staging of plays. In these contentions lawyers were frequently involved, as elders of the kirk representing their parishes.

The legal Establishment, safeguarded by the Treaty, was

more complex than the religious, and nearly as pervasive in influence, especially for the trend-setting groups. In 1758 the leading jurist of England, Blackstone, in his inaugural lecture at Oxford, commented that on the Continent of Europe a gentleman of education normally studied the *Institutes* of Justinian and the local constitutions of his own country, and "in the northern parts of our own island, where also the municipal laws are frequently connected with the civil, it is difficult to meet with a person of liberal education who is destitute of a competent knowledge in that science which is to be the guardian of his natural right and the rule of his civil conduct." The philosopher Hume, for example, was well read in law, and served as judge advocate on an amphibious campaign; Scott was sheriff of Selkirkshire, and held a near-sinecure as clerk of session in Edinburgh.

Scots law, not long before 1707, had received a comprehensive restatement by a great institutional writer, Sir James Dalrymple, Viscount of Stair, whose mental grasp reminds one of Aristotle. A recent head of the Scottish Bench, Lord Cooper of Culross, writes of Stair: "The publication of his *Institutions* in 1681 marked the creation of Scots Law as we have since known it—an original amalgam of Roman Law, Feudal Law and native customary law, systematised by resort to the law of nature and the Bible, and illuminated by many flashes of ideal metaphysics. . . . the resort still occasionally made to Stair in the House of Lords and the Privy Council suggests that it is not only in the estimation of his fellow-countrymen that he falls to be ranked among the great jurists of all time."

47

In dedicating to King Charles II, in 1681, his *Institutions of the Law of Scotland*, Stair has a passage that is a classic formulation of the type of nationalism endorsed by the leading Scots of the eighteenth century also: "We do not pretend to be amongst the great and rich kingdoms of the earth; yet we know not who can claim preference in antiquity and integrity, being of one blood and lineage, without mixture of any other people, and have so continued above two thousand years; during all which no foreign power was ever able to settle the dominion of a strange Lord over us, or to make us foresake our allegiance to your Majesty's royal ancestors, our native and kindly kings. . . .

"This nation hath not been obscure and unknown to the world; but the most famous nations have made use of our arms, and have still, in grateful remembrance, retained trophies and monuments of our courage and constancy. There be few wars in Christendom wherein we have not had considerable bodies of soldiers, regimented and commanded by themselves, and ofttimes general officers commanding them and whole armies of strangers, with great reputation and gallantry, which did advance them above the natives of those countries where they served. Neither have we wanted the fame of learning, at home and abroad, in the most eminent professions, divine or human. And as everywhere the most pregnant and active spirits apply themselves to the study and practice of law, so those that applied themselves to that profession amongst us have given great evidence of sharp and piercing spirits, with much readiness of conception and dexterity of expression; which are necessary qualifications both of the bench and bar, whereby the law of this kingdom hath attained to so great perfection, that it may, without arrogance, be compared with the laws of any of our neighbouring nations. For we are happy in having so few and so clear statutes. Our law is most part consuetudinary, whereby what is found inconvenient is obliterated and forgot. Our forms are plain and prompt, whereby the generality of the judicious have, with little pains, much insight in our law, and do, with the more security, enjoy their rights and possessions."

Stair later remarks: "We do always prefer the sense to the subtilty of law, and do seldom trip by niceties or formalities."

The central professional judiciary, the Court of Session, or College of Justice, had been established in 1532, and consisted of fifteen judges, its head being called the Lord President. Until 1808 they all sat together on important civil cases; but minor cases, and matters of evidence and procedure, were handled by one of their number, sitting singly. After some experiments, in 1825 it became the practice to divide the Court of Session into an Inner House, of two permanent groups of four, sitting separately, and an Outer House, where seven judges sat singly as Lords Ordinary. Under the Treaty the House of Lords in London took appeals from the Court of Session, in civil cases. There was no appeal to Westminster in criminal cases, which were finalized by the High Court of Justiciary, as established in 1672. Its nominal head was, until 1830, a nobleman favored by the king, and he needed no legal training. His style was Lord Justice General. The working head was the Lord Justice Clerk, who in civil matters stood second to the Lord President. Five Senators of

49

the College of Justice served as Commissioners of Justiciary. They also went on circuit, to Glasgow and other head burghs, and sat on important criminal cases, singly, but with a jury of fifteen men, who found by majority verdict and were not required to find unanimously. In 1815 jury trial was introduced into civil cases, to suit the convenience of the House of Lords, accustomed to English civil jury procedures; and a separate Scottish Jury Court functioned from 1815 to 1830, when it was merged in the Court of Session. Scots lawyers have never ceased to complain of civil jury trial, as a disadvantageous intruded Anglicization. There were also Commissary Courts, from 1563 to 1823, handling consistorial causes, about divorce, nullity, and such matters. From 1707 to 1856 there operated a Scottish Court of Exchequer, dealing with Crown revenues. The Scottish Court of Admiralty survived until 1830, when its civil and criminal powers were merged in the Court of Session and High Court of Justiciary, its prize jurisdiction having been merged in 1825 in the English Court of Admiralty. It will be apparent that the many official positions in and around these courts were useful to political jobbers, like the second and third Dukes of Argyll and Harry Dundas. But there were also local jobs. In each county the sheriff was endowed with important civil and criminal jurisdictions. The heritable local jurisdictions, a relic of feudal law, were abolished in 1748. Yet another central court was that of the Lord Lyon King-of-Arms, final authority on chieftainship and heraldry, and for the marshaling of state processions. His office is believed to have come down from Celtic times. On a very different level, the old Celtic legal system is said to have survived in such a custom as hand-fasting, a probationary period of cohabitation before marriage, a frequent condition being that the provisional wife should bear a male child within a year and a day of the contract. Another type of Scots marriage was by consent, exchanged between a man and a woman with genuine matrimonial intent, valid without writing or witnesses, if there were later corroboration, such as statements to relatives. As Lord Neaves put it,

> *Suppose that young Jocky or Jenny*
> *Say* "We two are husband and wife,"
> *The witnesses needn't be many.*
> *They're instantly buckled for life.*

The Crown's interest was represented by the Lord Advocate, aided by the Solicitor General for Scotland, and the Advocates Depute. In sheriffdoms the public prosecutor is styled Procurator Fiscal, a title recalling the large element of Roman law in Scots law. The original Celtic law had taken in elements of Anglic and Norman systems, and under the *Auld Alliance* with France there had been a growing reception of the Graeco-Roman civil law. Until 1560, Scots commonly went to France for legal studies, but from 1600 to 1800 mostly to the Netherlands. In that period some 1,600 Scots studied at Leiden, and others at Utrecht, including James Boswell, who, however, found many things to distract him from legality. The Faculty of Advocates controlled entry to the profession, by entrance tests in civil law (1619) or Scots law (1692). Since 1424 provision had been made for poor persons to have legal aid. Only Advocates could plead in the supreme courts; but in Sheriff Courts litigants could be represented by law agents or notaries public. The highest corporation of these, the Writers to His Majesty's Signet, had a fine library of their own. The Solicitors before the Supreme Courts, styled for short "S.S.C.," obtained a charter in 1797. Their legal training was greatly improved by a succession of professorial chairs in the University of Edinburgh in the eighteenth century, with incumbents mainly trained in Holland. In the Advocates' Library, of which Hume was Keeper (1752–57), most of the 1,500 legal tomes were Continental. Thus the trend-setting upper class had a cosmopolitan outlook, not insular or Anglicized.

In briefly introducing Scots law to the International Bar Association, in *International Bar News* (1961), the leading authority, Professor T. B. Smith, remarked that "Scots law, with its European and civilian background, latterly influenced by English law, stands, like the systems of Ceylon, Quebec, Louisiana, and South Africa, at the crossing of the two highways of legal thought." He states that, at the time of the Union, Scots private law was much more developed than English, in such matters as contract, delict (tort), unjust enrichment, and family law. He further writes: "Scottish criminal law reached maturity later than Scottish private law, and thus avoided premature rigidity and harshness. Even in the late 18th and early 19th century capital punishment was rare. . . . Liberal doctrines developed by Scottish judges regarding insanity, diminished responsibility and provocation have very recently been incorporated by statute into the criminal law of England. . . . Criminal prosecution in Scotland is essentially a public duty, not a private right, though, in very rare cases, leave may be given for private prosecution. The pivot of the administration in Scotland is the Lord Advocate, and it is he, or his Deputes, who decide whether to prosecute, the crime to be charged, the appropriate Court, and the procedure, whether summary or on indictment, to be followed. In each Sheriffdom Procurators-Fiscal responsible to the Lord Advocate exercise a delegated authority subject to his control."

The Lord Advocate, himself a political appointment by the London government, was the real ruler of Scotland in Scott's time. There had been also a Secretary of State, from 1707 to 1725 and 1741 to 1746; but after 1746 the Lord Advocate was undisputed master in all matters, not only legal. He was a Member of Parliament, in the House of Commons, where an Aberdeenshire M.P., Ferguson of Pitfour, remarked: "The Lord Advocate should always be a tall man. We Scotch members always vote with him, and we need, therefore, to be able to see him." Judges were appointed on his advice, and it seems clear that the administration of justice was not invariably as good as the Scots law that was being administered. Boswell, in a pamphlet of 1780, accuses the judges of levity, carelessness, partiality, indecorum, pecuniary shabbiness, and other faults. Of the head of the judiciary, Blair, who died in 1811, Scott wrote: "His integrity and legal knowledge joind to a peculiar dignity of thought action and expression had begun to establish in the minds of the public at large that confidence in the regular and solemn

administration of justice which is so necessary to its useful-
ness and respectability." Evidently the public had previously
lacked confidence in the judiciary. Judges being political ap-
pointments, at times of political excitement some of them
might give way to political antipathies. A notorious case was
in 1752, when James Stewart of the Glen was tried for com-
plicity in the murder of a Campbell. The Duke of Argyll,
chief of Clan Campbell, as Lord Justice General, presided in
Inveraray, head burgh of the Campbell territory, with eleven
men of the jury of fifteen surnamed Campbell. That was in
the backwash of the 1745 Jacobite Rising. Another discredit-
able period was in the 1790's, when the excesses of the French
Revolution had exacerbated feelings. The most illustrative
instance is the trial of Thomas Muir for sedition.

In common with many in England and Ireland, some
thinking Scots had sympathized with the first manifestations
of the French Revolution. In 1789 a Whig Club at Dundee
had sent congratulations to the French National Assembly,
hoping that "the flame you have kindled will consume the
remains of despotism and bigotry in Europe." The poet
Burns sent them four naval guns. James Maitland, eighth
Earl of Lauderdale, went to Paris and exhorted the mob in
defense of liberty; he was called "Citizen Maitland." Lord
Sempill contributed six thousand pairs of shoes for the
French Soldiers of Liberty. Members of the nobility and
gentry celebrated the Fall of the Bastille at public dinners in
Edinburgh, Glasgow, and Dundee. The ideas of Tom
Paine's book, *The Rights of Man,* got abroad; a Gaelic trans-
lation ran through the Highlands. Its official suppression as

seditious publicized it further. But as the French Revolution become more extreme, the upper classes took fright more and more, and became repressive. And the economic hardships of the period pressed on the poor. A Corn Law in 1791 imposed duties on imports and gave bounties to exporters, raising the cost of living. In Edinburgh a mob rioted, smashed the Lord Advocate's windows, and had to be fired on by soldiers and marines. The harvest of 1792 was a bad one, and misery increased with dearth. There had meantime grown up a Society of Friends of the People, based in London, to petition Parliament for "equal political representation and shorter parliaments." In Scotland its moving spirit was Thomas Muir of Huntershill (1765–99), son of a Glasgow merchant who had become laird of a near-by estate. He had been expelled from the University of Glasgow for siding with a professor of *avant-garde* views, and had become a member of the Faculty of Advocates, though his original intention had been to become a minister of the kirk. He served as an elder in Cadder parish. After a period of agitation in the country, he organized in December, 1792, in Edinburgh a Convention of the Friends of the People, at which he insisted on reading an address from the United Irishmen, a body regarded by the London government as dangerously treasonable. The Irish revolutionary nationalists there said: "We rejoice that you do not consider yourselves as merged and melted down into another country, but that in this great national question you are still Scotland, the land where Buchanan wrote, and Fletcher spoke, and Wallace fought."

On January 2, 1793, Muir was arrested on a charge of sedition, but liberated on bail. He went, via London, to Paris, arriving on January 20, the day before Louis XVI was guillotined. Within a fortnight the French Republic had declared war on Great Britain, which delayed Muir's return. He was declared an outlaw, and his name removed from the Faculty of Advocates. By an American ship he reached Ireland, and thence came to Scotland, where he was at once arrested. He was tried on August 30, 1793, for making seditious speeches, circulating seditious books and papers, and reading the seditious address of the United Irishmen to the Edinburgh Convention. In his defense Muir said: "So far from inflaming the minds of men to sedition and outrage, all the witnesses have concurred that my only anxiety was to impress upon them the necessity of peace, of goodwill, and of good morals. What, then, has been my crime? Not the lending to a relation a copy of Mr. Paine's works; not the giving away to another a few numbers of an innocent and constitutional publication; but for having dared to be, according to the measure of my feeble abilities, a strenuous and active advocate for an equal representation of the people in the House of the people; for having dared to attempt to accomplish a measure, by legal means, which was to diminish the weight of their taxes, and to put an end to the profusion of their blood. From my infancy to this moment I have devoted myself to the cause of the people. It is a good cause. It shall ultimately prevail. It shall finally triumph."

The Lord Justice Clerk, Lord Braxfield, presiding, disregarded the "indecent applause" that broke out, and began his summing up to the jury of fifteen men, picked by himself from a list of forty-five. He stated that the British Constitution was the best in the world. "Is not every man secure in his life, liberty, and property?" He referred to the spirit of sedition and revolt in the previous winter. "I leave it for you to judge whether it was perfectly innocent or not in Mr. Muir, at such a time, to go about among ignorant country people, and among the lower classes of the people, making them leave off their work, and inducing them to believe that a reform was absolutely necessary to preserve their safety and their liberty. . . . Mr. Muir might have known that no attention could be paid to such a rabble. What right had they to representation? He could have told them that Parliament would never listen to their petition. How could they think of it? A Government in every country should be just like a Corporation: and, in this country, it is made up of the landed interest, which alone has a right to be represented; as for the rabble, who have nothing but personal property, what hold has the nation of them? What security for the payment of their taxes? They may pack up all their property on their backs, and leave the country in the twinkling of an eye, but landed property cannot be removed."

Next day the jury found Muir guilty, and the judges unanimously sentenced him to transportation for fourteen years to Australia. He arrived there in October, 1794, with three others, Palmer, Skirving, and Margarot, of the Friends of the People. The poet Burns had subscribed his guinea to their organization, and it was under the stress of the feelings aroused by Muir's trial that he wrote his national anthem, "Scots, wha hae wi' Wallace bled . . . ," a versification of what he imagined to have been Bruce's address before Bannockburn:

> *Wha for Scotland's King and law*
> *Freedom's sword will strongly draw,*
> *Freeman stand, or freeman fa'?*
> *Let him follow me!*

Thomas Muir was rescued from Australia in January, 1796, by an American ship, the *Otter*, of Boston, Massachusetts, which took him to Vancouver Island, where he transferred to a Spanish ship for San Blas, end of a route from the Pacific to Mexico City. The Spaniards, alarmed by his association with French revolutionaries, put him on a Spanish frigate bound for Cadiz. He was wounded in an action with a British man-of-war, but reached Spain, and from there went to Paris, as a guest of the French Directory, who consulted him about proposals for invading Britain. In 1798, British Intelligence listed him as one of a proposed Directory for Scotland. But the invasion was shelved. Muir retired to Chantilly, and was found dead on January 26, 1799. His memory, and that of his fellow political martyrs, helped to inspire the movement that carried the Reform Bill of 1832.

The growing conflict of classes, and horizontal division of the nation, revealed by Braxfield in Muir's trial, were intensified in the period after 1815. But if the liberal-minded judge, Lord Cockburn, is correct, in the 1790's "the lower orders seemed to take no particular concern in anything." Cockburn and his reforming friends were, he states, extremely few; and, "belonging mostly to the bar, they were constantly and insolently reminded that the case of their brother Thomas Muir, sentenced for sedition, was intended for their special edification." The Tory party, during the years of Scott's blossoming as a poet and novelist, "engrossed almost the whole wealth, and rank, and public office, of the country, and at least three-fourths of the population. . . . As to our Institutions—there was no popular representation; all town-councils elected themselves; the Established Church had no visible rival. . . . The wishes of the people were not merely despised, but it was thought and openly announced, as a necessary precaution against revolution, that they should be thwarted." Cockburn gives an instance, soon after 1800, during the heyday of Tory reaction, where the seat-holders of a town church applied to government, which was the patron, for the promotion of the second clergyman on the death of the first minister. A member of the Cabinet wrote that "the single fact of the people having interfered so far as to express a wish was conclusive against what they desired; and another appointment was instantly made." Reactionaries went so far as to consider trousers "Jacobinical," in contrast to knee breeches, and natural hair subversive, since upholders of the Constitution ought to wear powdered wigs.

Cockburn, who was a nephew of Henry Dundas, and knew politics from the inside, summed matters up thus: "With the people put down and the Whigs powerless, Government was the master of nearly every individual in Scotland, but especially in Edinburgh, which was the chief seat of its influence. The infidelity of the French gave it almost all the pious; their atrocities all the timid; rapidly-increasing taxation and establishments all the venal; the higher and middle ranks were at its command, and the people at its feet. The pulpit, the bench, the bar, the colleges, the parliamentary electors, the magistracies, the local institutions, were so completely at the service of the party in power, that the idea of independence, besides being monstrous and absurd, was suppressed by a feeling of conscious ingratitude. Henry Dundas, an Edinburgh man, and well calculated by talent and manner to make despotism popular, was the absolute dictator of Scotland."

Considering the history of Scottish Presbyterianism in the seventeenth and nineteenth centuries, students have often wondered at the ascendancy of the Moderates in the eighteenth. Their characteristics were satirized by the Rev. John Witherspoon, who later became the only clerical signatory of the American Declaration of Independence, and president of the College of New Jersey, which became Princeton University. Five editions appeared between 1753 and 1763 of his *Ecclesiastical Characteristics: Or, The Arcana of Church Policy*. Among thirteen maxims to attain the repute of a Moderate Man, one may note Maxim X: "A minister must endeavor to acquire as great a degree of politeness, in his carriage and behaviour, and to catch as much of the air of a fine gentleman, as possibly he can." Maxim IV sets out "special marks and signs of a talent for preaching. 1. His subjects must be confined to social duties. 2. He must recommend them only from rational considerations, viz. the beauty and comely proportions of virtue, and its advantages in the present life, without any regard to a future state of more extended self-interest. 3. His authorities must be drawn from heathen writers, none, or as few as possible, from Scripture. 4. He must be very unacceptable to the people."

Typical of the Moderate clergy was the Rev. Dr. Hugh Blair, who defended David Hume's skepticism in a letter to Professor James Beattie of Aberdeen, who had attacked Hume in a best-selling *Essay on the Nature and Immutability of Truth; In Opposition to Sophistry and Scepticism* (1770). Blair argued: "In some places I cannot help thinking you are too severe on Mr Hume; & perhaps indeed from my partiality to the Worthy, humane, good natured man, I wish you had been less so. . . . I have not altogether those formidable Views which you entertain of the Consequences of Scepticism. It may prove dangerous, to be sure, and it is right to combat it: the Ballance should always be kept hanging in the right side; but a little fluctuation, now and then, to the sceptical side, tends perhaps to humble the Pride of Understanding, and to check biggotry; and the consequences as to practice, I am enclined to think, are not very great."

Hume's skepticism had been very much a public issue since 1748, when he published his essay *On Miracles*, with its suave conclusion: "So that, upon the whole, we may conclude, that the *Christian Religion* not only was at first attended with miracles, but even at this day cannot be believed by any reasonable person without one. Mere reason is insufficient to convince us of its veracity: And whoever is moved by *Faith* to assent to it, is conscious of a continued miracle in his own person, which subverts all the principles of his understanding, and gives him a determination to believe what is most contrary to custom and experience."

Hume's skepticism had started when he was aged about eighteen, in his thinking about causation. Mossner writes: "In the Age of Reason, Hume set himself apart as a systematic anti-rationalist. Most of what passes for knowledge, he taught, is not achieved by the faculty of reason but by custom and habit; and most knowledge is not perfectly certain, but, at best, probable. The realm of reason is, therefore, restricted to the relations of ideas, as in pure logic and pure mathematics. . . . All other knowledge belongs to the realm of matter of fact. . . . And all our knowledge of matter of fact is determined by our inferences from cause to effect." To pursue the argument in Hume's words: "No matter of fact can be proved but from its cause or its effect. No thing can be known to be the cause of another but by experience. We can give no reason for extending to the future our experience in the past; but are entirely determined by custom, when we conceive an effect to follow from its usual cause. But we also believe an effect to follow, as well as conceive it. This belief joins no new idea to the conception. It only varies the manner of conceiving, and makes a difference to the feeling or sentiment. Belief, therefore, in all matters of fact arises only from custom, and is an idea conceived in a peculiar *manner*."

Hume's contemporaries seem not to have grasped his main point, but it had a delayed reaction when it woke from his dogmatic slumbers Immanuel Kant, a German allegedly of Scots descent; and today philosophers still argue seriously about Hume's notions of causation. The hostility of Scots ministers to his skepticism prevented his receiving the chair of Moral Philosophy in Edinburgh (1745) and the chair of Logic at Glasgow (1752). Thus Scotland's greatest philosopher never taught in any university. But, in attempts to answer his skepticism, there arose what came to be known as "the Scottish Philosophy of Common Sense," which in turn influenced the church. Its founder, Thomas Reid, professor of Philosophy at King's College, Aberdeen, from 1752, joined in founding in 1758 the Aberdeen Philosophical Society, which, he wrote to Hume, "is much indebted to you for its entertainment. Your company would, although we are all good Christians, be more acceptable than that of St. Athanasius; and, since we cannot have you upon the bench, you are brought oftener than any other man to the bar, accused and defended with great zeal, but without bitterness." Reid succeeded Adam Smith in the Glasgow chair of Moral Philosophy in 1764, when also he published his *Inquiry into the Human Mind on the Principles of Common Sense*. Reid's pupil, Dugald Stewart, propagated the "Common Sense" philosophy in Edinburgh, as professor of Moral Philosophy, from 1785, having among his pupils the founders of the *Edinburgh Review* in 1802, Sydney Smith, Brougham, Jeffrey, and Francis Horner; and such diverse types as Sir Walter Scott, James Mill, the future Prime Ministers Lord John Russell and Lord Palmerston, and Dr. Thomas Chalmers, leader of the Disruption of the Church of Scotland in 1843. In the 1830's Scottish "Common Sense" became the basis of academic instruction in philosophy in the France of Louis

Philippe, a nation still in many respects the center of European civilization. For most of the nineteenth century it dominated the American universities; and its influence is detected in the philosophies of C. S. Peirce, Rosmini, G. E. Moore, and the Louvain Ontologists.

This philosophy impinged on Scottish law and church affairs in the latter part of Scott's life, when a growing evangelical movement, accompanied by the rise of an industrial wage-earning class and an urban proletariat living in misery, led to new demands that the choice of parish ministers should be taken from landowners and vested in congregations. For, according to the "Common Sense" theory, there is in human consciousness a sense, a primitive vision of the whole, that is common to all persons. General Assemblies of the church heatedly argued the cognitive capacities of the plain, untutored citizen, when the issue was whether the lairds' choice of minister could be vetoed by the men of the congregation, either for reasons stated or without any statement of reasons. Dr. Chalmers declared that he found something almost divine in the attitude of a cottage patriarch who could instinctively feel his disapproval of a presentee but could not explain it. A generation earlier, in 1805, the same Dr. Chalmers, not yet a perfervid Evangelical, had written that, "after the satisfactory discharge of his parish duties, a minister may enjoy five days in the week of uninterrupted leisure for the prosecution of any science in which his taste may dispose him to engage." There one sees the worldly outlook of the Moderates, who dominated for most of the age of Hume and Scott. Yet, though they dominated, they were

64

challenged, every now and then strongly, by the Evangelical, or Wild, party. In the 1750's the Wild waged a pamphleteering war on David Hume and his friend Henry Home, Lord Kames, and extended it to include the Rev. John Home, minister of Athelstaneford, who had written a tragedy, *Douglas*. At the General Assembly of 1756 the Committee of Overtures brought in a resolution, or overture, for a committee to enquire into the writings of "one person, styling himself *David Hume, Esq.*, who hath arrived at such a degree of boldness as publicly to avow himself the author of books containing the most rude and open attacks upon the glorious Gospel of Christ, and principles evidently subversive even of natural religion and the foundations of morality, if not establishing direct Atheism." The young advocate Alexander Wedderburn, later to become Lord High Chancellor of Great Britain, and Earl of Rosslyn, led the defense of Hume initially; and the attack failed. The attack on the heretical opinions of Lord Kames fizzled out in the Presbytery of Edinburgh, but the 1757 General Assembly gave some satisfaction to the evangelical Highfliers by recommending to presbyteries to take care "that none of the ministers of this Church attend the Theatre." It was soon dead-lettered. Dr. Alexander Carlyle, minister of Inveresk, known as "Jupiter" for his godlike deportment, was a chief target of attack for backing Home's *Douglas*; but he was able to note in his *Autobiography* "that in the year 1784, when the great actress Mrs. Siddons first appeared in Edinburgh, during the sitting of the General Assembly, that court was obliged to fix all its important business for the alternate days when she did not act, as all the younger members, clergy as well as laity, took their stations in the theatre on those days by three in the afternoon."

Incidentally, it is a sign of the Anglicization of the Moderates that Carlyle writes of "clergy" and "laity." For in Calvinist Presbyterianism there is no such distinction; Cardinal Bellarmini, the Roman Catholic theologian, noted that Protestantism abolished the distinction between clergy and laity. Anglicization had existed in language from the 1560's, when an English version of the Bible was adopted; and ministers preached and prayed in English, with a Scots accent. The congregational singing, too, was in English, in metrical versions, which Scott in 1818 refused to help in amending. He wrote to the Rev. Principal Baird of Edinburgh University: "The expression of the old metrical translation though homely is plain forcible & intelligible and very often possesses a rude sort of majesty which perhaps would be ill exchanged for more elegance. Their antiquity is also a circumstance striking to the imagination & possessing a corresponding influence upon the feelings. They are the very words and accents of our early reformers sung by them in woe in the fields in the churches and on the scaffold. The parting with this very association of ideas is a serious loss to the cause of Devotion and scarce to be incurd without the certainty of corresponding advantages. But if these recollections are valuable to persons of education they are almost indispensible to the edification of the lower ranks." It may be noted that Scott, himself by this time long habituated to attending with his wife the Episcopalian chapel, still wrote of the Presbyterian service as "our national worship." These metrical Psalms were sung without accompaniment. Pennant comments on St. Giles' that, "There is no music either in this or any other of the *Scotch* churches, for *Peg* still faints at the sound of an organ. This is the more surprizing, as the Dutch, who have the same established religion, are extremely fond of that solemn instrument; and even in the great church of *Geneva* the Psalmody is accompanied with an organ." Buzonnière thought the Presbyterian singing compared favorably with that in French Roman Catholic churches. The system was that the precentor sang each line solo, and the congregation repeated it, either in unison or with whatever concord or discord each individual might produce under the influence of the Holy Spirit. Men wore their bonnets, or hats, during the sermon but doffed them for the prayers and the singing. Communion was received sitting, not kneeling, the communicants being placed at a long table from the pulpit to the main door. In rural areas parishes usually combined for communions, which made mass meetings, attended by much drinking and other distractions, depicted by Burns in *The Holy Fair*.

Buzonnière was amazed that the congregation sat and chatted while awaiting the arrival of Dr. Chalmers. He also remarked that the Scottish Sunday was divided into two parts: "During the daytime the streets near the churches are encumbered with a crowd of the faithful going to the services, Bible under arm, and plunged in the most edifying self-communion; in the evening one risks being overturned at every pace by some of those good Christians who, instead of abandoning themselves to profane joys, have been peaceably meditating in the taverns upon the exhortations of their ministers." That was in 1827. A few years later the *Scotsman* newspaper remarked: "That Scotland is, pretty near at least, the most drunken nation on the face of the earth is a fact never quite capable of denial. It may seem strange that Edinburgh, the headquarters of the various sections of a clergy more powerful than any other save that of Ireland, should, in respect of drunkenness, exhibit scenes and habits unparalleled in any other metropolis." One cause of this drunkenness was the shift, after the Union of 1707, from ale, with low alcoholic content, to whisky, a strong distillation. In 1708 only 50,844½ gallons of whisky had been distilled, whereas in 1783 the Lowlands had distilled 1,000,000 gallons, and the Highlands 696,000. In the same period the amount of two-penny ale that had paid duty had sunk from 288,336 barrels to 97,577½. Creech complained: "Ardent spirits, so easily obtained, are hurtful to the health, industry, and morals of the people." The mischief undoubtedly grew during Scott's later lifetime, to reach its height about 1850.

There are various indications of the fluctuations of religious fervor during the period. Cockburn found that, from about 1750, the rise in relative wealth of the other classes tended to lower the status of parish ministers. Further, "Principal Robertson's ecclesiastical policy tended to divide our ministers into two classes; one, and by far the largest, of which had no principle superior to that of obsequious allegiance to patrons; the other, devoting itself entirely to the religion of the lower orders, had no taste or ambition for anything higher than what that religion required, or could, to ordinary minds, suggest. The old historical glory had faded; and, under the insignificance of repose, it was chiefly a lower description of men who were tempted to enlist in the ecclesiastical service. The humbleness of their livings, and even the well-meant cheapness of their education, vulgarised them still more; so that learning and refinement, being scarcely attainable, ceased to be expected." Sir Walter Scott, in a similar tone, writes to Lord Montagu, who was controlling the patronage of the young Duke of Buccleugh: "One of the Dukes Black cattle has departed this life vizt. the Minister of Sanquhar and I am cap in hand with a suit for George Thompson my domestic tutor if there is no previous engagement or preferable claim. I have just sent Charles to an English school and my Scotch Abraham Adams for such this worthy creature is both in learning and simplicity is now in the wide world." Ministers might retort that it was better to be considered "Black cattle" than black sheep. Yet in 1817 Scott's friend Lady Louisa Stuart was writing: "I am glad you are so indifferent about the wrath of the *Unco Guid*, as Burns calls them. You have no notion what a strong and increasing body they are in this country." Cockburn, at the time of the Reform Bill of 1832, found: "Religion is certainly more the fashion than it used to be. There is more said about it; there has been a great rise, and consequently a great competition, of sects; and the general mass of the religious public has been enlarged." In 1835–36 a parliamentary commission reported on the average number of persons attending places of worship in Edinburgh, thus: "Established 20,419; United

Secession, Relief, Burghers, &c. [all Presbyterian sects] 15,793; Baptists, Independents, &c. 5,220; Episcopalians 3,327; Catholics 2,750; Methodists 1,470; Unitarians 150; Society of Friends 100; Jews 20 families."

This competition of sects improved the Established church ministers. One of their duties was poor relief, a matter of great interest to the English reformer William Cobbett, in his tour of 1832. He wrote: "The distribution of the alms being committed to their exemplary parochial ministers, a great deal is done to alleviate the sufferings of the destitute." He found, however, that "seceders have generally the most able and most diligent ministers." Ability consisted mainly in power to preach. Thus Cockburn comments on the seceder Mr. Struthers, who attracted "persons of good taste, not of his community, to his church merely for the pleasure of hearing him preach. . . . in the Circus, a place of theatrical exhibition at the head of Leith Walk. It was strange to see the pit, boxes, and galleries filled with devoted worshippers, and to detect the edges of the scenes and other vestiges of the Saturday night, while a pulpit was brought forward to the front of the stage on which there stood a tall, pale, well-dressed man, earnestly but gently alluring the audience to religion by elegant declamation." Wholly different types could exist, even in the Establishment, like Mr. James Lapslie of Campsie, of whom Scott's son-in-law J. G. Lockhart wrote: "He is a fine, tall bony man, with a face full of fire, and a bush of white locks, which he shakes about him like the thyrsus of a Bacchanal. He tears his waistcoat open—he bares his breast as if he had scars to show—he bellows—he sobs—he weeps—

and sits down at the end of his harangue trembling all to the fingers' ends like an exhausted Pythoness." The Town Council of Edinburgh having spent a good deal of money in repairing churches, and building the great church at the west end of George Street, St. George's, with a dome 150 feet high, launched a policy of putting in ministers who could attract a congregation willing to pay rents for regular seats. Thus they hired the Rev. Dr. Andrew Thomson, of whom Cockburn relates: "His Whig reputation was so odious, that it rather seemed at one time as if civic beggary would be preferred to it; and most vehemently was his entrance into our untroubled fold opposed. But, after as much plotting as if it had been for the Popedom, he got it, and in a few years rewarded his electors by drawing about £1800 a year for them; a fact which, of itself, loosened all the city churches from the dead sea in which they were standing." The Whig Dr. Thomson shocked the loyal in 1817 by refusing to hold a service on a weekday for the death of Princess Charlotte. By contrast, when George IV sought to divorce his wife Queen Caroline, and issued an order forbidding prayers for Her Majesty, then, as Cockburn records, "the Presbyterians, who own no earthly head, kicked. Our whole seceders, and a great many of the established clergy, including of course Andrew Thomson, to whom the blunder was delightful, disdained this mandate, and prayed for her the more fervently that her husband's ministry declared that she was wicked." Politics would keep creeping in, as when the Rev. Sir Henry Moncreiff prayed for George IV on the first Sunday after his accession: "And, O Lord, stablish his heart in righteousness, and in the principles of the glorious revolution of sixteen hunder and echty echt." On similar lines, when Prince Charles Edward was in Edinburgh in 1745, an old minister prayed: "O Lord, this young man who has come among us seeking an earthly crown—grant him a heavenly one."

Creech noted that in 1763, "Sunday was strictly observed by all ranks as a day of devotion," but in 1783, "Attendance on church is much neglected: Sunday is made a day of relaxation: Families think it ungenteel to take their domestics to church with them: The streets are often crowded in the time of worship; and, in the evenings, they are shamefully loose and riotous. Family worship is almost totally disused, and is even wearing out among the clergy. . . . Visiting and catechising are disused, except by one or two of the clergy: if people do not chuse to go to church, they may remain as ignorant as Hottentots, and the Ten Commandments be as little known as rescinded acts of parliament." Earlier in the century ruling elders, as well as the minister, had a duty to visit families, to see that children knew their Catechism, to censure vices of the parents, and to pray for the sick. Scott as a boy was examined by his father every Sunday evening on the contents of the day's sermons. Alexander Somerville, author of *The Autobiography of a Working Man*, tells how his father, a poor farm-servant, conducted family worship nightly: he prayed; the family sang a Psalm; he read a chapter from the Bible, and ended with an extempore prayer. On Sunday evenings he would smoke—the rest of the week he chewed tobacco, a practice more thrifty than smoking it—

72

and listen to one of the family reading a sermon. When Somerville went to Edinburgh, it was his greatest "intellectual treat" to hear Dr. Andrew Thompson. He writes also of the ambition with which he saved up for a new suit of Sunday clothes, and regards it as a laudable object for a wage earner to be "superiorly dressed on a Sunday." He goes on: ". . . since I have been in towns where public parks are instituted, and facilities are afforded for recreation out of doors, I see nothing in those parks more beneficial than this—that they induce working people who have the means, and who previously wasted their means in dirt and drunkenness within doors, to be clean, to be well-dressed, to care for their families being well-dressed; and, above all, to care for themselves being well behaved, and to go out like honest and good men, and look the world honestly in the face." Dressing up for church attendance was discussed by ministers contributing to the Statistical Account, one of them dilating also on feminine hair styles: "Formerly, their hair flowed in easy ringlets over their shoulders; not many years ago, it was bound behind into a cue; now, it spreads into a protuberance on the forehead, supported by cushions; sometimes it is plain, and split in the middle. But who can describe the caprice of female ornament, more various than the changes of the moon?"

In the 1790's country parishes still employed the "stool of repentance" for the public censure of members of the congregation, especially those detected in fornication. Some exacted fines instead of, or in addition to, exposing the guilty parties to the public view on one or more Sundays. But in

Edinburgh, Creech laments that, in 1783, even church censure of adultery was obsolete. "Women who have been rendered infamous by public divorce have been permitted to marry the Adulterer," and even known adulteresses were received into society, "notwithstanding the endeavours of our worthy Queen to check such a violation of morality, decency, the laws of the country, and the rights of the virtuous." The fines collected by the kirk treasurer for bastard children amounted in 1763 to £154, but in 1783 they were nearly £600. Another fluctuation in the effective impact of the church appears from statistics on brothels. A soldier of Cumberland's army in 1746 discovered "vast Numbers of Bawdy-Houses" in the Canongate alone; but in 1763, Creech says, "There were about six or seven brothels or houses of bad fame in Edinburgh, and a very few only of the lowest and most ignorant order of females skulked about at night." Only one of "the impure tribe" could afford a silk gown, and she died mad. But in 1783, he goes on, "The number of brothels and houses of civil accommodation are increased to some hundreds," and "Gentlemens and citizens daughters are upon the town." It was a feature of Calvinism as popularly understood among many Scots that grace, not works, was what mattered for salvation. Before the world began, God, through his inscrutable mercy, chose some men for eternal salvation, without any regard for their foreseen merits in life; he left others to eternal damnation. Calvin was not alone among the Reformers in holding this doctrine, advanced already by St. Augustine and by Scholastic theologians; but it had accidentally become emphasized by controversy. Thus

74

a minister reports the case of a "whimsical but pious old man," who, "from his extreme humility, and mistaken respect to the doctrines of grace, resolved to abandon the practice of good works for six weeks, lest, as he said, he should be tempted to boast of them alone, to the dishonour of his Maker, as if meriting at the hands of God." The minister concludes: "Of his having adhered to his resolution, a female domestic gave to the world, about nine months after, a living and pregnant proof." James Hogg dealt with this aspect of popular Calvinism in his novel, *The Private Memoirs and Confessions of a Justified Sinner*. And Burns, in *Holy Willie's Prayer*, satirizes a tendency to hypocrisy often enough found among the "Unco Guid." An excessive fondness for controversial divinity, or theological disputation, is a charge brought against some of their flock by ministers; and this was a feature of the General Assembly too, as in 1805, in the discussion of the case of John Leslie, who had published in 1804 *An Experimental Enquiry into the Nature and Properties of Radiant Heat*. He was later to be the first man to achieve artificial congelation, and may be regarded as father of all our refrigerators. But in 1805 what he caused was heat. The Moderate ministers wished to put into the vacant chair of Mathematics in the University a Rev. Dr. Macknight, but Leslie was backed by leading scientific men. However, in his book he had written: "Mr. Hume is the first, as far as I know, who has treated of Causation in a philosophical manner." The cry of atheism was raised. The Presbytery of Edinburgh claimed a right to veto Leslie's appointment. The Synod referred the issue to the Assembly, which debated the matter for two days, finding for Leslie. Among the disputants was the head of the Bench, Lord President Campbell, and a prominent politician, Lord Lauderdale.

But most typical of the ebullitions of this Edinburgh culture of church and law was the intervention of a judge, Lord Hermand. Cockburn writes: "Hermand was in a glorious frenzy. Spurning all unfairness, a religious doubt, entangled with mystical metaphysics, and countenanced by his party, had great attractions for his excitable head and Presbyterian taste! What a figure! as he stood on the floor declaiming and screaming, amidst the divines—the tall man, with his thin powdered locks and long pigtail, the long Court of Session cravat flaccid and steaming with the heat, and the obtrusive linen! His most memorable words were: 'Sir! I sucked in the being and attributes of God with my mother's milk!'"

Such excitement was, however, not the rule for most of Scott's period, but rather a firm earnestness in adherence to principles. Thus, in 1814, when a meeting was held against West Indian slavery, the Rev. Sir Henry Moncreiff got up a petition to Parliament, signed by some 12,000 persons. Lord Cockburn and Thomas Erskine of Linlathen had charge of a copy of the petition for signature in the Grassmarket, where Covenanters had been executed in days when the church was ruled by bishops, whom the people regarded as merely the police agents of Papist kings. The petition included a reference to "Lords Spiritual," in the House of Lords, meaning bishops. Cockburn and Erskine "were both surprised to find a piece of Calvinistic Whiggery, which we thought had faded, still deeply seated. Many who signed the petition to the Commons shrunk back from one to the Lords. They could not get over the 'Lords Spiritual.' No reasoning could reconcile them to the title. 'I would rather not homologate [agree]' was the general and conclusive answer." But the earnest adherence to principle did finally, in 1843, boil over on the issue of the right of the congregation to "call" its minister, when over four hundred ministers of the Church of Scotland left their parishes, and their homes and incomes, to form the Free Church of Scotland. Lord Cockburn, who did not join them, called this "the most honourable fact for Scotland that its whole history supplies." And Lady Nairne, the poetess, daughter of the old Jacobite laird Oliphant of Gask, sold her family silver to help endow the Free Kirk. Here was a triumph for the enthusiasm and democracy so long derided.

5

Sciences and Arts

WHEN SCOTT WAS AT HIS PRIME, Edinburgh was at its zenith as a center of civilization. Among the factors causing this was the exclusion of all the British from the Continent during the Napoleonic wars, so that Edinburgh became a substitute resort for an educational Grand Tour. Further, since England had only two universities and Ireland one, and admission to them involved subscription to Anglicanism, many English, Welsh, and Irish Nonconformists had already for decades come to Scottish universities, and especially to Edinburgh. The chief attractions seem to have been the scientific teaching in the medical faculty, and the philosophical and literary criticism in that of arts. Cockburn notes, about 1805 to 1820, "the blaze of that popular literature which made this the second city in the empire for learning and science; and the extent, and the ease, with which literature and society embellished each other, without rivalry, and without pedantry." Statistics show that the University had its maximum of matriculated students, during Scott's lifetime, in 1815, when the total was 2,097. Of these, 757 studied literature and philosophy; 178, divinity; 233, law; and 929, medicine. Medicine was thus the biggest faculty, and was regarded as a general scientific education. Only 76 graduated in medicine in that session. Maybe others found it too difficult. Besides, one could buy an M.D. degree in Scotland's senior university, St. Andrews, as the French revolutionary Marat had done.

The University of Edinburgh had been founded in 1582, more or less on the model of Calvin's reformed University of Geneva, as a municipal institution with a royal charter. Its first medical professor, in 1685, was Sir Robert Sibbald, who had promoted the Royal College of Physicians of Edinburgh (1681). Its members had the exclusive privilege of practicing medicine in Edinburgh. From 1505 there had been a corporation of surgeons and barbers, and from 1657 a reformed corporation of surgeons and apothecaries, excluding barbers. This in 1778 became the Royal College of Surgeons, which gave a diploma. Sibbald's more famous contemporary, Dr. Archibald Pitcairne (1652–1713), originally trained as a lawyer, became professor of medicine at Leiden in 1692, and taught Hermann Boerhaave, eminent in medicine and chemistry, some of whose pupils in turn built up the Edinburgh faculty. Pitcairne was a skillful Latin versifier and an ardent Jacobite. He sat daily in a tavern, treating the poor for nothing. In 1721, Alexander Monro, the first of three of the name, became professor of anatomy, and four other medical professors were appointed, who taught a systematic course. Already for half a century Sir Thomas Burnet's *Thesaurus Medicinae* (1673) had been the best-selling medical textbook of Europe; and one finds that systematization was a line in which Edinburgh usually excelled. Monro the First promoted in 1731 the *Philosophical Society of Edinburgh*, to publish essays on medicine and surgery. In 1737 its scope was broadened to take in mathematics, philosophy, and literature. David Hume served as its secretary from 1751 for some years. In 1783 it became, by royal charter, the Royal Society of Edinburgh, and still functions today as a focus for scientific and other work in Scotland. Alexander Monro the Second (1733–1817) discovered the "foramen of Monro," between the lateral ventricles of the brain, and his son held the same chair. A more remarkable dynasty of savants was that of the Gregory family, originally from Aberdeenshire, who had sixteen university professors in three generations. James Gregory (1638–75) had been a coinventor, with Newton and Leibnitz, of the calculus. John Gregory (1724–73) held the chair of medicine at Edinburgh, and was succeeded by his son James Gregory (1753–1821), noted for a staple family medicine, "Gregory's Mixture." His son Duncan Farquharson Gregory (1813–44) became a distinguished algebraist. The practical bent of Edinburgh's medical men is exemplified in William Cullen (1710–90), who held the chair of chemistry (1755) and then that of the theory of physic (1766). He was the first to produce a rational catalogue of *materia medica*, and wrote works setting out the principles of general medicine. He also pioneered in agricultural chemistry and the study of soils and manures. One sees here how Edinburgh and its university were integrated in the economic revolution of the century, being the headquarters for the improving lairds.

Cullen's successor in the chemistry chair, Joseph Black (1728–99), son of a Scots wine merchant at Bordeaux, had described in his M.D. thesis of 1754 the formation of carbon dioxide. His work led to the eventual rejection of the phlogiston theory, which had been impeding the progress of chemistry. Later his name became famous in the fields of latent heat and specific heat. Black was actively involved in the early Industrial Revolution, financing James Watt to the tune of £1,000 for experiments with steam engines. He founded the first chemical society in the world, and so early as 1766, to amuse friends at a dinner party, sent up a balloon filled with hydrogen. Reading of his experiments induced the Montgolfier brothers in France to make the first balloon ascent, in 1783.

Among the pioneers of the discrimination of gases was Sir Walter Scott's uncle, Daniel Rutherford (1749–1819), who discovered the difference between carbon dioxide and nitrogen. He served as professor of botany, not of chemistry—one more indication how little compartmentalized were the academic researches of that era. His father had been professor of medicine. One notes a good many family successions. For instance, John Hope (1725–86) held the chair of botany, and was a pioneer of vegetable physiology; his son Thomas Charles Hope (1766–1844) professed chemistry, and discovered the element strontium, named from a Highland place, Strontian. Among medical men, Andrew Duncan the Elder (1744–1828), professor of the Institutes of Medicine, pioneered the humane treatment of lunatics, in a public asylum (1792–1807). His son Andrew Duncan the Younger (1773–1832) held the chair of medical jurisprudence, but owed his distinction to the isolation of cinchonine. Old Andrew Duncan popularized sea-bathing at Leith, and had the habit, even when over eighty, of climbing Arthur's Seat on the First of May, and, as Cockburn puts it, "celebrating the feat by what he called a poem." He also presided over the Caledonian Horticultural Society.

Among the medical men who made some sort of notable advance in their art were William Smellie (1697–1763), in obstetrics; Robert Whytt (1714–66), in the study of the sympathetic nervous system; Sir John Pringle (1707–82), in antiseptics; William Hunter (1718–83), in gynecology; Sir Charles Bell (1774–1842), whose anatomy of the brain and investigation of the functions of the nervous system made him the chief founder of neurology; James Syme (1799–1870), pioneer of plastic surgery; Sir James Young Simpson (1808–59), a pioneer in the use of chloroform and other anesthetics; and John Goodsir (1814–67), professor of anatomy, a pioneer student of the cell nucleus. It was to him that Virchow dedicated his more celebrated theory in this field. For those curious in Edinburgh heredities, Goodsir was great-grandfather of the leading Edinburgh poet of our current century, Sydney Goodsir Smith. Robert Louis Stevenson, Edinburgh's finest writer in the century following Scott, likewise belonged to a dynasty of scientific eminence. Robert Stevenson (1772–1850) was engineer to the Board of Northern Lighthouses, in which Scott took a keen interest, sailing round Scotland in one of their ships. This Stevenson invented flashing intermittent lights, and the hydrophore, for taking samples of water at various depths. His son Alan (1807–65) used prismatic rings in the light-condensing system. Son David (1815–86) devised for Japan an "aseismatic" type of lighthouse to resist earthquakes. Finally, Thomas Stevenson (1818–87) developed the azimuthal condensing system for lights, and begat the poet and novelist Robert Louis Stevenson, who was as proud of his family's lighthouses as of any Scottish achievement.

One ought to note the practical bent of most Edinburgh intellectual activity, coupled with considerable powers of innovation and imagination. Thus Francis Home (1719–1813), the first professor of *materia medica*, gave an impetus to the textile industry by using sulphuric acid as a bleaching agent; and promoted the study of plant nutrition in his *Principles of Agriculture and Vegetation*, where also he educated readers in hygiene. The boiling of drinking water as a precaution against epidemics was his idea. Geology was much advanced by James Hutton (1726–97), with his theory of the earth's formation. Born in Edinburgh and trained in Paris and Leiden, where he took his M.D. in 1749, his interest in practical farming and mining took him to Freiburg, to the mining school of Werner, who taught the "catastrophic" theory, that all changes in the earth's structure were due to great upheavals. Hutton's studies led him to propose a "uniformitarian" theory, taking account of the influence of rain, ice, and other factors, as well as of volcanic melting and extru-

sion. Hutton's theory was popularized in 1802 by John Playfair (1748–1819), professor of mathematics; and proved ex-
perimentally by Sir James Hall of Dunglass (1761–1832),
who melted rocks to see what happened. Many lairds were
keenly concerned with geology, like Sir George Stewart
Mackenzie of Coull (1780–1848), who proved the making
of diamonds from carbon, and Sir Charles Lyell (1797–1875),
whose *Principles of Geology* (1830–33) expounded for the
earth a theory of evolution, which largely prepared scientific
opinion for the theory of Darwin and Wallace about the
evolution of species.

Edinburgh was primarily the headquarters of an aristocratic landowning caste at this time. Cockburn remarks:
"There was no class of the community so little thought of
at this time as the mercantile. . . . They had no direct political
power; no votes; and were far too subservient to be feared.
The lairds were not merely more deferred to, but were in
the height of their influence. They returned thirty members
to Parliament, and had themselves and their connections in
all public positions of honour or of pay." Some younger sons,
to be sure, went into trade, as David Hume himself set off
for Bristol to work in the office of a sugar merchant. By the
accidents of death and succession, men bred as merchants or
lawyers might find themselves owning land. One way or
other, the gentry applied their wits and their connections to
unified resource development of their estates, operating from
winter headquarters in Edinburgh. The University term ran
from November to April, only the medical faculty having
some classes in May to July. From April to November the

upper classes of Edinburgh spent most of their time at country houses or traveling abroad. Many, too, were in the British
Army or Navy, and some of them made scientific contributions here too. For example, Archibald Cochrane, ninth Earl
of Dundonald (1749–1831), a considerable coal owner and
an Admiral, distilled tar and used it to preserve ships' hulls.
The London Admiralty refused to use it, and rejected
also his pioneer suggestion for an artificial smokescreen in
naval warfare. Incidentally, the famous naval manoeuver of
"breaking the line," which gained Rodney and others so
many famous victories, is claimed as the invention of a Scots
laird, John Clerk of Eldin. General Robert Melville (1723–
1809) invented the carronade, a precision gun for naval service (1759). Colonel Patrick Ferguson of Pitfour (1744–80)
patented the breech-loading rifle in 1776, and used it effec-
tively against the troops of George Washington, who, however, shot him in an ambush. Through the jealousy of his
superior officers, the use of his invention was discontinued.
The Rev. John Forsyth (1768–1843), a sporting parish minister, invented the percussion lock, about 1800, but the London government would not use it. Napoleon I offered him
£20,000 for the invention in 1807, but Forsyth patriotically
refused the offer. On the day of his death, thirty-six years
later, he received the first installment of a pension from the
London government. Somewhat comparable is the case of
the discovery, in 1756, by the Edinburgh physician James
Lind (1716–94) that lemon juice is the best specific against
scurvy. The London Admiralty resisted the idea for almost
forty years. Great improvements in the hygiene of the navy

were made by Gilbert Blane of Blanefield (1749–1834), who, for example, was the first to issue a free soap ration; and in that of the army by Henry Marshall (1775–1851), who also developed the statistical basis of military hygiene. The distillation of fresh water from sea water was a discovery of Dr. Lind, and several other Scots of the period applied their minds to the seas. John Rennie (1761–1821) was the leading builder of harbors and of bridges in his day. Thomas Morton (1781–1832) patented a slipway for launching ships, at Leith; and there too James Jardine (1776–1858) determined the mean level of the sea. This was of practical relevance to the building of a canal from the Forth to the Clyde, in fact from the North Sea to the Atlantic. The practical and statistical bent of Edinburgh intellectuals is seen once more in the fact that Edinburgh has the longest series of reliable weather records in the world, from 1731 to 1736, and then continuously from 1769 on.

In mathematics, pure and applied, the greatest name is Colin Maclaurin (1698–1746), son of a parish minister in Argyll. He became professor at Aberdeen at the age of nineteen, and moved to Edinburgh in 1725. He was celebrated for his treatment of fluxions, and gave his name to Maclaurin's Theorem. He attracted numerous pupils, many of whom held leading positions in the British artillery arm during the Seven Years' War. James Stirling of Garden (1692–1770) expounded the mathematics of summing an infinite series. John Robison (1739–1805) gave the first proof of the inverse square law in mechanics, and served as first secretary of the Royal Society of Edinburgh (1783). Sir David Brewster

(1781–1868) made advances in optics, inventing the kaleido-
scope, and was the main founder of the British Association
for the Advancement of Science (1831). Sir John Leslie
(1766–1832) developed the physics of heat and cold, being
the first man to make ice artificially. It is an odd by-product
of Edinburgh's phase as the "Modern Athens" that Peter
Nicholson (1765–1844), of Prestonkirk near by, discovered
that Greek moldings were conic sections, and that Ionic capi-
tals should be composed of logarithmic spirals.

A notable feature of the scientific advances of the age is
the participation in them of men of humble origin, who
had been given a chance by the parish schools stemming
from the Presbyterian system. For example, James Ferguson
(1710–76), son of a Banffshire farm laborer, made many in-
genious scientific instruments, including a tide dial and an
eclipsareon. James Short (1710–68) was the most celebrated
maker of telescopes in his century. John Brown (1735–88),
son of a Berwickshire laborer, was important in medical
history for his discrediting of the practice of bloodletting.
James Clark (1734–1806), farrier to the King in Scotland,
revolutionized the treatment of horses, by new methods of
shoeing, by study of the animal's pulse rate, and by insisting
on clean water and fresh air in stables. Thomas Telford
(1757–1834), son of a Dumfriesshire shepherd, constructed
the two greatest canals in the world at the time, the Caledonian across Scotland, and the Göta in Sweden. John Loudon
McAdam (1756–1836) revolutionized road-building. William Murdoch (1754–1839), son of an Ayrshire millwright,
applied gas from coal and peat to illumination, and, among

many other inventions, made a three-wheeled motorcar, worked by steam. Sir William Fairbairn (1789–1874), son of a Kelso farm servant, constructed the first iron steamship (1830). Robert Wilson (1803–82), son of a Dunbar fisherman, invented the first practical screw propeller (1826). The London Admiralty rejected it without testing.

As Edinburgh's printing industry was part of the basis for the city's reputation, it may be noted that stereotyping was invented in 1725 by an Edinburgh man, William Ged (1690–1749); but the vested interests in the trade stopped its application. Alexander Tulloch (1759–1825) developed it, and secured its acceptance. Type design was greatly advanced by Alexander Wilson (1714–86), who also improved the thermometer, pioneered in meteorology, and was the first to see that sunspots are cavities in the luminous matter round the sun. William Wallace (1768–1843), of Dysart, invented the eidograph for copying plans. It is interesting that Audubon (1785–1851) had his wonderful plates produced in Edinburgh, and that the first edition of the *Encyclopaedia Britannica* (1771) was edited in Edinburgh by William Smellie (1740–95). Among miscellaneous inventions or scientific break-through theories devised by Scotsmen alive in the years of Scott one may remark the first practical reaping machine, by James Smith of Deanston (1789–1850), who also invented the subsoil plow; the adhesive postage stamp, by James Chalmers (1782–1853); the first waterproofed fabrics, by Charles Macintosh (1766-1843), cousin of General Sir John Moore, of Corunna fame; limelight, by Thomas Drummond (1797–1840), son of an Edinburgh solicitor; the elucidation of the aurora borealis, by James Farquharson of Coull (1781–1843); the seismometer for measuring earthquakes, by James David Forbes (1809–68), who also pioneered the study of glacial flow; the cell nucleus and the Brownian movement, by Robert Brown of Montrose (1773–1858); the steam hammer, by James Nasmyth (1808–90); the first wrought iron girder bridge, by Andrew Thomson (1832); the pedal bicycle, by Kirkpatrick MacMillan (1813–78); Graham's Law concerning the rate of diffusion of gases, by Thomas Graham (1805–69); and such useful appliances as the India-rubber tire and the fountain pen, both invented by Robert William Thomson, of Stonehaven (1822–73). Some of the many scientific personalities mentioned spent much or most of their time in London or elsewhere outside Scotland, but the basis of their intellectual formation lay in the type of culture focused on Edinburgh. Here there had been eager receptivity for what was best in foreign ways of thinking; and the same is true for the arts.

The Flemish and Dutch connections continued to be influential in the period after 1603, but Italy too became a magnet for Scots artists: for example, George Jamesone, John Michael Wright, William Gouw Ferguson, and David Paton. After the Union of 1707, Italy came to dominate, in painting and architecture alike. Thus William Aikman of Cairney (1682–1731) sold his family estate to make a long tour in Italy, with trips to Constantinople and Syria (1707–12). John Smibert (1684–1751), after training in Italy, went to America in 1728, and influenced the New England school around Boston. In imitation of the Academy of St.

Luke in Italy, there was started at Edinburgh in 1729 a School of St. Luke. Its artist members included the young Allan Ramsay the painter (1713–84) and among the "Lovers of Painting" were his father Allan Ramsay the poet, and the architect William Adam (1689–1748), father of the famous Adam brothers. In the 1720's the chief patron among the Scots nobility was the second Marquis of Annandale (1688–1730), who got plans for architectural details direct from Italy, ignoring London. But most patrons and artists did not ignore London, which was yearly growing in eminence as a center of taste and of patronage. It is impossible to estimate the loss to Scotland by the removal of the royal court in 1603 and the parliament in 1707, with all the public and private patronage of the arts, and of manufactures, that accrue to a city which is fully a national capital. One may imagine what would happen if Queen Elizabeth, now reigning, were to transfer the main seat of her sovereignty to Ottawa, having regard to the fact that Canada has a vastly greater economic potential than the island of Britain. In a few generations, with Ottawa as the center of patronage, legislation, finance, and fashion, London would tend to become a provincial city, and its ablest artists and professional men would often be tempted to make their careers in Canada rather than in England. During the eighteenth century it became notorious, as Dr. Johnson gibed, that ". . . the noblest prospect which a Scotchman ever sees is the highroad that leads him to England!" Some strong spirits resisted the tide, like David Hume, who gave up living among what he termed "the Barbarians who inhabit the Banks of the Thames," and returned to the "very sociable, civilized people" of Edinburgh.

Some talented Scots, as usual, went farther afield than London. One of the more remarkable is Charles Cameron, who became the favorite architect of Catherine the Great of Russia, after having enjoyed the patronage of Lord Bute, the first Scots premier of Britain, and having written a book on the baths of the Romans. Classical archaeology, indeed, was a leading source of inspiration to Scots in this age. It could even be pursued in parts of Scotland, as in the near neighborhood of Edinburgh by the painter Aikman's cousin, Sir John Clerk of Penicuik, whose family fortune had been derived from trade in Paris a century before. George Drummond, the Lord Provost of Edinburgh, who mainly planned the New Town, had been secretary to the laird of Penicuik. Besides patronizing the Adam family, the Clerks had elaborate ceiling and wall paintings done, on Ossianic and Scottish historical themes, by Alexander Runciman (1736–85), after his years of study in Rome. The Scot most fully identified with Italy was Gavin Hamilton of Murdostoun (1723–98), who spent most of his life at Rome, digging up Hadrian's villa at Tivoli, and forming collections of Greek and Roman sculpture, which were visited by Scots patrons and artists. In his own neoclassical paintings he anticipates Jacques Louis David, though without so high an accomplishment. The Scots vagrant habits may be observed in Cosmo John Alexander (1724–72), who got his first name from Cosimo de' Medici, Grand Duke of Tuscany, patron of his father, John

Alexander. Cosmo John studied in Rome and went to America before 1770. He there taught Gilbert Stuart (1754–1828), the Scoto-American portrayer of George Washington and others.

Highest in quality and versatility was Allan Ramsay the painter, who studied in Rome and Naples, then settled in Edinburgh, where he founded in 1754 the Select Society, with David Hume, Adam Smith, Lord Kames, and other leading men. It met in the Advocates' Library on Wednesday evenings in the months from November to August, and debated various topics, before being regaled with "warm suppers and excellent claret." Practical and theoretical advances resulted in many fields from the contact of souls in this convivial "brain trust." Of Allan Ramsay, Dr. Johnson stated: "You will not find a man in whose conversation there is more instruction, more information, or more elegance." He is best remembered as a painter, especially successful with women; and he became a court painter to George III and his wife, who enjoyed, among his other talents, his ability to talk to them in German. But he took more seriously, for much of his life, his writings and classical studies, for example his excavations for Horace's Sabine farm near Tivoli. An obituary in *The Gentlemen's Magazine*, for August 10, 1784, says: " . . . the polite and literary world have sustained an irreparable loss, as few men have exceeded him in correctness of taste, brilliancy of wit or soundness of understanding. . . . His publications are numerous and various; several of them are on political subjects, in which is displayed much useful knowledge of the constitution of this country, for which he was ever a strenuous and disinterested advocate." The all-roundness of these leading Scots is one of their striking features, and the scientific bent of the nation is reflected in their painting. Dr. Stanley Cursiter, currently Her Majesty's limner for Scotland, remarks on William Millar, one of the more ordinary artists active in the 1750's, that "He belongs to the 'warts and all' class of painters; but this is typical of Scottish portraiture as it gradually came to assume a more definitely Scottish character. Something Calvinistic . . . may lie at the bottom of it." Dr. Cursiter finds "a sort of grim satisfaction in analysing the sitter with all the thoroughness of a post-mortem." Allan Ramsay tempers this scientific objectivity with a gentlemanly courtesy, the spirit of Burns's maxim:

Then gently scan your brother man,
Still gentler sister woman.
Though they may gang a kennin wrang ["go a bit wrong"],
To step aside is human.

It is often noted that Allan Ramsay's style would be fully at home in his contemporary France; but in fact Italy dominated for him, as for most Scots of the period. However, when the Board of Manufactures set up, in 1760, its Trustees' Academy, its first two heads were Frenchmen. Then in 1772 they appointed Alexander Runciman, who had spent seven years in Italy. With his Swiss friend Henry Fuseli, he was inclined to put ideas above technique, and Sir James Clerk gave him scope at Penicuik House. With patriotic enthusiasm, and emulating Michelangelo, he painted Ossian harping to an enraptured throng by the sea, under a fantastic sunset. Episodes from the Ossianic poems were represented in compartments of the large coved ceiling, as were the four great rivers, Tay, Spey, Clyde, and Tweed. At Penicuik, also, he did on a staircase cupola scenes from the life of St. Margaret of Scotland, with landscapes of Edinburgh and the Forth. Imagination is somewhat rare in Scottish painting, which makes the more regrettable the fire that destroyed Runciman's chief work, in 1899. Subject paintings, however, now became fashionable, as with David Allan (1744–96). He worked in Rome and London, and, on return to Edinburgh, exploited local subjects, such as fishwives, water carriers, or the Lord High Commissioner's procession to the General Assembly of the Kirk, and social customs, like the Penny Wedding, at which guests brought contributions to the bridal feast both for their own entertainment there and to help the young couple to set up house. His contemporary, John Kay (1742–1826), a working barber, was Scotland's finest caricaturist, and etched about nine hundred plates, prints from which sold at a penny each. At the opposite extreme was Jacob More (1740–93), who spent the last twenty years of his life in Rome, painting dramatic landscapes, which were admired by Reynolds and Goethe.

Portraits, however, were the Scottish main interest. There were two talented ladies in this field: Catherine Read (1723–78), a fine pastelist, latterly in India; and Anne Forbes (1745–1834), granddaughter of William Aikman. Archibald Skirving (1749–1819), an exciseman in Edinburgh, gave up his civil-service post in middle life, to spend ten years in Rome; and could command one hundred guineas for a head in pastel, more than many established artists could get for a portrait in oils. He did a fine head of his fellow exciseman, the poet Burns, but not from life. David Martin (1737–98), Allan Ramsay's chief assistant, became painter to the Prince of Wales, later George IV. But the finest in this work was Sir Henry Raeburn (1756–1823). The son of a millowner and yarn boiler at the village of Stockbridge, at the foot of the north slope of the New Town, he was a younger son, and sent to Heriot's Hospital, the charitable school founded by James VI's jeweler, a French-style château, which the Englishman Pennant thought "too magnificent for educating poor children." Raeburn was then apprenticed to a goldsmith, and began copying miniatures. Later he copied pictures for David Martin, who, however, never showed him how to prepare materials. In his early twenties he married a lady twelve years older than himself, Ann Edgar, widow of Count James Leslie, and had the disposition of her fortune and estate of Deanhaugh. Thus he was essentially a self-taught amateur painter. He made trips to London and Rome, only to return more than ever self-confident in his own style. He had a studio built in York Place, and worked there on a regular routine. After breakfasting at eight, he walked up the hill to the studio, and painted from nine to five, treating four sitters for up to two hours each, discoursing to them on topics like mechanics and shipbuilding. Then he went home to dine at six. He also played golf and dined out, and finally died from a chill caught while on an archaeological trip with Sir Walter Scott. The fashionable London painter Sir Thomas Lawrence said of Raeburn's portrait of a Highland chief, *The McNab*, that he had never seen a finer representation of a human being. Sir Isaiah Berlin, on the other hand, when shown round the Scottish galleries by the present writer in 1938, was naughty enough to remark that "Raeburn painted men as if they were stags." The truth is that some of his customers were rather like stags, and that Raeburn suddenly lost £17,000 in 1807 through involvement in a shipping venture of his brother-in-law, so that he had to do a lot of work for money, the same incentive as stimulated so much of Scott's output of novels. Yet even the most run-of-the-mill Raeburns have a sterling craftsmanship; and not even the dullest client could complain of ill usage. At his best, Raeburn can give an astonishingly direct and frank statement of what a person looked like, and at heart was like.

In 1808 a Society of Artists was formed to hold exhibitions, some of which took place in Raeburn's gallery, attached to his studio. In 1819 there was started an Institution for the Encouragement of the Fine Arts, which ran loan exhibitions of Old Masters, and added contemporary work in 1821. By a breakaway from it there was founded in 1826 a Scottish Academy, and the two bodies held rival exhibitions and formed rival collections. In 1829 they united, to form what now flourishes as the Royal Scottish Academy. By this time the dominant taste was for large historical pictures, like those of Sir William Allan (1782–1850), who traveled in Russia and the Near East. His one-man show of 1814 attracted the support of Scott, who promoted this type of painting. Typical was Allan's *Murder of Rizzio,* the Italian secretary of Mary

Queen of Scots. The most permanently interesting in this genre was Sir David Wilkie (1785–1841), who was mainly influenced by the Dutch domestic tradition. His father was minister of Cults in Fife, where the son made drawings in the kirk on Sunday, and did a tableau of *Pitlessie Fair*, with 140 figures, among them that of his reverend father conversing with the local publican, or keeper of a drinking den. In London from 1805, Wilkie enjoyed the most eminent patronage. For his canvas of 1822, *Chelsea Pensioners Reading the Gazette of the Battle of Waterloo*, the Duke of Wellington paid him 1,200 golden guineas, cash down, saying that he did not want his banker to know what a damned fool he was. Wilkie became King's limner for Scotland, in succession to Raeburn, and painted George IV in Highland dress, which had been proscribed by the London Parliament under George II. Wilkie was an excellent etcher, as was his friend Andrew Geddes (1783–1844). Scotland's finest engraver was the Jacobite Sir Robert Strange (1721–92), an Orkneyman, who engraved, among other things, the bank notes issued by Prince Charles Edward in 1745. He spent most of his life in France and Italy. A Scot who went to neither, but attained the first excellence in his medium, was James Tassie (1735–99), a mason who sculptured gravestones and the like. In 1760 he was stimulated by the exhibition held in Glasgow University by the brothers Robert and Andrew Foulis, admirable printers, who were running an academy on an Italian model. Tassie took to modeling in a fine vitreous paste, or enamel, both in order to reproduce Greek and Roman

97

gems and to make portraits of contemporaries. After experiments with Dr. Quin in Dublin, he settled in London in 1766.

Among architects the lead was taken by the Adam dynasty. William Adam (1689–1748) had visited France and the Netherlands, but can hardly be reckoned higher than an eminently practical builder, who would carry out a job to the taste of his patron. He worked for the Board of Ordnance, which built some fine forts; and he was familiar with the architectural publications of the period. His own style is a Palladian influenced by Vanbrugh and James Gibbs, the Aberdonian Scot who did some of the best buildings at Oxford and Cambridge. But one can also see a flavor of the Scottish castles of the sixteenth and seventeenth centuries, with their exuberant ornament. Among his clients was the second Earl of Hopetoun, brother-in-law of Annandale, Scotland's leading patron in the 1720's. Hopetoun's son Charles Hope went with Robert Adam (1728–92) on his Grand Tour, starting in 1754. Previous to that, Robert and his brother James, four years younger, had worked in their father's office, which was then engaged, among other projects, on the Duke of Argyll's Neo-Gothic castle at Inveraray. It is interesting that, in 1754, when Allan Ramsay did a portrait of James Adam, he at first held a Neo-Gothic plan, which was later replaced by a Palladian design. Italian influence reinforced this preference, but every now and then one or other of the Adam brothers would try another Neo-Gothic experiment. A better knowledge of the best Greek work was being gained in the 1750's, with Stuart and Revett in Greece, preparing the first volume of their *Antiquities of Athens* (1755). Excavations at Pompeii, also, from 1755, enlightened students about a later stage of Greek building; and a pedantic Neo-Hellenism began to arise. When Robert Adam saw Stuart's work at Spencer House, in London, he remarked that the ceilings might be "Greek to the teeth," but, "by God, they are not handsome." James Adam, on his Grand Tour, took a notion of the "clever Greek wines, such as intoxicated Anacreon and fuddled Sappho"; but neither Robert nor James aimed at any sort of Hellenist purism. They became partners in London, where Robert had become royal architect to George III in November, 1761. The result of their tours, and detailed study by one or other of such sites as Diocletian's palace at Spalato, was to fill their heads with what they termed "proper ornaments." Robert referred to Rome as his "Holy See of Pleasurable Antiquity," and it is worth noting how much the Scots were at home there then. They had a Caledonian Club, which used the old Court Scots, "our ain Mither tongue"; and on St. Andrew's Day, 1756, the Earls of Elgin and Rosebery entertained their compatriots with a sea of liquor. This sort of cultural nationalism is part of the background of the "Adam style." In a design for a new building for the United Kingdom parliament, Robert writes: "I have taken care that North Britain shall bear its own share in all decorations." That means, more or less, that one must have a thistle for every rose; but, on a less superficial level, the Adam style derives from the sense of "the picturesque," which had been powerfully promoted in the eighteenth century by James Thomson, the poet of *The*

Seasons, and in a different way, by Macpherson's *Ossian*. Robert Adam was laird of a property in Kinross-shire, with the old castle of Dowhill; and something of the castellate Scottish tradition keeps cropping up in his buildings. Robert felt that his genius would be "thrown away upon Scotland," for lack of enough rich patrons to put his noble thoughts into execution; but even in the rich London neighborhood Robert was often restricted to new schemes of interior decoration for fabrics already built by others. Thus the Adam style has tended to be regarded as primarily a matter of superficial ornamentation. In reaction against his father's exuberance, Robert's decoration is elegant, tending to understatement. For exteriors, the Adams' great interest was picturesque movement: "Movement is meant to express the rise and fall, the advance and recess, with other diversity of form, in the different parts of a building, so as to add greatly to the picturesqueness of the composition." This was a romantic advance from classical Palladianism.

Sir William Chambers (1723–96) was a rival, and opponent, of Robert Adam. He came of a Scots family in Gothenburg, Sweden, but spent part of his youth in Yorkshire, before going in the service of the East India Company to India and China, with occasional visits to Scotland and England. His early formation as an architect was at Paris, though he later spent longer in Italy. Enjoying the patronage of George III, he did most of his work in England, in a severer style than the Adams, but with occasional lighthearted excursions, like the Pagoda at Kew Gardens. He was Roman,

and anti-Greek, in taste. In Edinburgh his best work was
Sir Laurence Dundas' house in St. Andrew's Square.

An interesting dynasty of architects was that of Mylne, several of whom were hereditary Royal Master Masons, from
the late fifteenth century. Thomas Mylne, city surveyor of
Edinburgh, had two sons, Robert (1733–1811) and William
(1734–90), who went to Rome, mostly on their own feet, and
lived there in the 1750's on £30 a year. William designed the
first North Bridge in Edinburgh, of which part collapsed,
with loss of life, before it was finished (1769); he proceeded
to Ireland, and became engineer to the Dublin waterworks.
Robert Mylne, who won the Papal medal at the Academy
of St. Luke in 1758, built the delightful concert room, St.
Cecilia's Hall, between the High Street and Cowgate, on the
model of the Parma Opera House. Most of his work was
done in London, and he was buried in St. Paul's there.

Architecture and painting were among the interests of another remarkable family, the Nasmyths. Alexander Nasmyth
(1758–1840) belonged to a family who had been builders in
Edinburgh for generations. He himself was apprenticed as
a coach-painter, when Allan Ramsay observed his talent, and
arranged to break his indentures and train him as his own
assistant in London. In 1778 he returned to Edinburgh, and
found a patron in Patrick Millar of Dalswinton (1731–1815),
a Dumfriesshire laird, who leased to the poet Burns the
farm of Ellisland. He was also a director of the Carron
ironworks, and exploited Nasmyth's mechanical aptitudes.
Nasmyth and Burns were on board Symington's prototype

steamship when it first sailed on the Dalswinton loch in 1788. Nasmyth made money by portraits, and married a sister of Sir James Foulis of Woodhall; he did a lot of excellent landscape painting, especially after 1793, when his Radical politics made conversation with Tory sitters embarrassing; and he laid out many parks around country houses. He devised the method of sowing seed of trees on inaccessible hill-faces by firing them from cannon. In Edinburgh he designed the delightful St. Bernard's Well temple of Hygieia, on the Water of Leith (1789), at the expense of a judge, Lord Gardenstone, who combined an elegant architectural taste with the cozy habit of having a real live pig to warm his bed. Patrick Nasmyth (1787–1831), Alexander's son, became a popular landscape painter in London; and six of Alexander's daughters painted more or less well. James Nasmyth (1808–90) invented the steam hammer, a flexible shaft for drills, a hydraulic punching machine, and other devices, and made some astronomical discoveries. He left his fortune for necessitous artists in Scotland. Among Alexander Nasmyth's pupils was the Rev. John Thomson, minister of Duddingston (1778–1840), son of an Ayrshire minister. He painted romantic seascapes, and was a friend of Walter Scott. His parish lay just south of Arthur's Seat, and he combined his pastoral duties with a lucrative output of painting, by the expedient of calling the studio in the manse garden "Edinburgh," so that his housekeeper could truthfully inform unwanted callers that "The Minister is in Edinburgh."

A comparable versatility and pluralism, often lighthearted, is to be found when one turns to survey the Scottish men of letters of this age.

6

Literature and Journalism

History, songs, essays, and sociability were the dominant influences in forming the Scottish contributions to literature up to the death of Walter Scott, and he himself fully reflects them all. "Noo there's ane end of ane auld sang," said the Chancellor, the Earl of Seafield, after signing the act ratifying the Treaty of Union, in the last session, so far, of the Scots Parliament. But the removal of Scots parliamentarians to London proved to be by no means the end of the old Scots songs, nor an inhibition to the production of new and even better songs. Indeed, the challenge to the long historic tradition of separate nationality, implicit in the Union of 1707, evoked a response, especially in literature, that continues today.

One of the leading personalities in the survival of Scots literature was himself half-English, Allan Ramsay the poet (1686–1758). His father, John Ramsay, was land agent for the Earl of Hopetoun, and manager of his lead and gold mines in the hills of Lanarkshire; but he died in 1685, and the poet never knew him. His mother, Alice Bower, was daughter of an English engineer, from Derbyshire, who had been brought up to start Lord Hopetoun's mines. She married, as second husband, a local farmer, Andrew Crichton; and it was in this mixed Anglo-Scottish household that Allan Ramsay grew up. He was thus aware from childhood of the differences of vocabulary and expressive power in the Scots and English languages. Later he quite deliberately sought to fuse them, thinking thereby to have a more copious and expressive medium of utterance, for instance, as he writes, the ability to say "an *empty* house, a *toom* barrel, a *boss* head, and a *hollow* heart." After some schooling at Leadhills to the age of fourteen or so, his mother having died, he was sent by his stepfather to Edinburgh, and apprenticed to a wigmaker. In 1709 he became a burgess, and set up shop as a master wigmaker. In 1712 he married a lawyer's daughter, Christian Ross, and begat the future painter Allan Ramsay, who was followed by at least seven other children. He also joined the Easy Club, a literary group, for "Mutual Improvement in Conversation." The members used pseudonyms, and at first Ramsay had an English one, Isaac Bickerstaff; but he changed that a year later to Gavin Douglas, the early sixteenth-century Bishop of Dunkeld, whose Scots version of the *Aeneid* had been reprinted at Edinburgh in 1710, by Thomas Ruddiman (1674–1757), David Hume's predecessor as Keeper of the Advocates' Library, and a chief promoter of sound Latinity and the maintenance of the national culture. It is notable that already as a boy in Lanarkshire, Ramsay had read books, according to his son, "such as were then in

the hands of the country people all over Scotland," for example, "the History, in verse, of King Robert the Bruce, the
exploits of Sir William Wallace, and the poems of Sir David
Lindsay." Lindsay's satires against the corrupt Romanist
clergy before 1560 were orally current, and there were many
chapbooks peddled round villages commemorating the heroes of the War of Independence. Burns in his turn drew
inspiration from similar sources. In Edinburgh there had
appeared James Watson's *A Choice Collection of Comic and
Serious Scots Poems* (1706–11), which made available, without music, a fairly representative selection of older Scots
verse in various styles, along with a good deal of English,
some of it contemporary, and versions from Latin. Its first
poem was *Christ's Kirk on the Green*, a genre piece about
a folk merrymaking, ascribed to James V, father of Mary
Queen of Scots. In 1718, Ramsay reprinted this piece, anonymously, on broadsheets, with extra verses by himself in colloquial or archaic Scots. He also began to issue contemporary
verses for occasions about the town, in the current Scots
spoken by all, high and low, about local characters who kept
tippling houses, brothels, and so forth. In 1721 he produced
his first collection, dedicated "To the most Beautiful, the
Scots Ladies." In the preface he remarks: "The *Scotticisms*,
which perhaps may offend some over-nice Ear, give new Life
and Grace to the Poetry, and become their Place as well as
the *Doric* dialect of *Theocritus*, so much admired by the best
Judges." Here we have the dichotomy, which persists, between English as the language of prose, as it were Attic, and
Scots as a medium for certain kinds of verse, like the Doric

of the pastoral and other mimes of Theocritus. Indeed, a fashion arose of using "Doric" to mean the Scots tongue. It is notable that among the subscribers to Ramsay's volume were the
poet Pope and the essayist Steele. The wits of early Georgian
London relished considerably Scotch, as well as Irish and
Welsh, national idiosyncrasies; and this taste continued until
quite recent times. Though a wigmaker's shop was rather
a good center for the distribution of occasional verses, Ramsay made enough money by his book to abandon wigmaking
and set up as a bookseller. After some moves, he fixed his
business in the Luckenbooths, a centrally sited block, looking
down the High Street. His sign was the heads of William
Drummond of Hawthornden and of Ben Jonson. Jonson, a
Londoner of Scots extraction, had been the guest near Edinburgh of Drummond, one of the courtier class who, after
James VI's shift to England in 1603, had cultivated verse in
English. Drummond had also written a history of the earlier
Stewarts, and a macaronic poem in a mixture of Scots and
Latin, the *Polemo-middinia, or Middenfecht*, which was still
a favorite recitation item at Edinburgh medical graduation
parties in Scott's day. These heads perhaps symbolized the
Anglo-Scottish culture for which Ramsay stood. A born pub-
licist, Ramsay established also, about 1725, what is thought
to have been the first circulating library in Great Britain. It
grew to some thirty thousand volumes. Robert Wodrow, the
Presbyterian historian, lamented: "Profaneness is come to a
great height; all the villanous, profane and obscene books
and plays printed at London by Curll and others are got

down by Allan Ramsay, and let out for an easy price to young boys, servant boys, servant girls of the better sort, and gentlemen, and vice and obscenity are dreadfully propagated." Ramsay himself issued a pastoral drama, *The Gentle Shepherd*, with Scots songs interspersed, which became a favorite also in England (1725); after John Gay, who became his friend, had produced *The Beggar's Opera* (1728), Ramsay remodeled his play to be more like Gay's. Here again one sees the Anglo-Scottish compromise. In the same spirit he issued his anthologies, *The Tea Table Miscellany* (1724–32), artfully associating old and new Scots pieces with old and new English ones, so that he could appeal to a wider public and please various tastes in the same household. *The Ever Green* (1724) helped to make known some of the finest old Scots poetry, until then buried in the Bannatyne manuscript. As a public relations officer for a Scottish renaissance, Ramsay was masterly. He indicated the tunes to which poems were to be sung, and we know that fashionable ladies cultivated singing of Scots songs as a social accomplishment. They sang, unaccompanied, as they sat at the tea-table, or after supper. It seems that the harp, formerly used in Scotland, was currently not much practiced, nor the spinet and harpsichord; and the pianoforte did not come in until about 1770. From the 1720's there were many volumes of Scots songs issued, with or without tunes or instrumental settings, at Edinburgh, London, Paris, and elsewhere. As the century progressed the Italian influence in setting dominated, though Burns and others protested against an excess of Italian "tirliewhirlies." Burns contributed pieces to George Thomson's *Select Collection of Original Scotish Airs*, with "symphonies" and accompaniments for violin and piano by Pleyel, Kozeluch, and even Haydn and Beethoven. Some purists contended that these eminent foreign musicians distorted the native idioms; but the majority of patrons seem to have felt that Scottish music was not a merely folkloristic manifestation, but something worthy of international attention with an *avant-garde* sophisticated presentation. This concern for a contemporary European, or an Anglicized, window-dressing of Scottish wares, in literature, is exemplified in Hume's histories and Scott's poems and novels. Ramsay was the most influential setter of the fashion.

Stage plays had been performed in Scotland since medieval guilds put on pageants; even John Knox had attended a stage play. But the association of the Covenanters with the English Puritans had broken the tradition. Irregular visits by touring companies had done something to revive interest, when Ramsay refitted, "at vast expense," the Carruber's Close Theatre, off the High Street, in 1736. Unfortunately, Walpole's licensing Act of 1737 made it possible for the Edinburgh magistrates, prompted by some of the "Unco Guid," to close the place down. The Act, however, did not prevent concerts being given for payment, and from 1742 it became a practice to append a play, free of charge, to a concert. From 1767 the theater became legally established. But in the result no important dramatists appeared untl Sir James Barrie and James Bridie in recent generations. Sir Walter Scott took a keen interest, but his plays were unsuccessful, though shows based on his novels were wildly popular for long enough. Burns had plans for patriotic Scots plays, but died too soon to realize them. John Home's tragedy of *Douglas* (1756) was put on in London in 1757, when an enthusiastic Aberdonian cried out, from the front of the shilling gallery: "Ou fie, lads, fat think ye o' yir Willy Shakespeare noo?" It held the boards in London for sixty years, and Shelley, when writing *The Cenci,* seems to have taken it as a model. Leading actresses, like Peg Woffington and Sarah Siddons, played the part of Lady Randolph, and thought it important and exacting, according to Dame Sibyl Thorndike, who writes of it: "It deals in a simple, direct fashion with the passions of mother-hood, jealousy, patriotism and covetousness. The characterization is strong and clear, and the writing, in firm, vigorous blank verse, is consciously a little pompous, to give it the grand manner. . . . the play should be regarded as nearer to the formal style of the Greek Tragedies, written as they were for large open-air theatres. . . . It more closely resembles the form and style of opera than the modern realistic play. . . . There is no doubt that in its day the emotional effect of the play was very great." David Hume took part in a rehearsal before the Edinburgh first night, with several Moderate ministers, in the presence of several judges; and claimed that John Home "appears a true disciple of Sophocles and Racine." Today the tragedy has failed to recapture a steady audience, and in Edinburgh of its own time it was not much more than a nine days' wonder. The public taste ran strongly towards ballad opera, rather than straight drama. Symptomatic was the production in 1769 of Arne's opera *Artaxerxes,* with three Scots songs added by the young Scots poet Robert Fergusson (1750–74), to be sung by the Italian Tenducci. Again, for Shield's *Rosina* (1784) the overture was embellished by a final march tune, where the oboe imitated the great Scots bagpipe, and the bassoons supplied the drones, the tune itself being a variant of that to which Burns later wrote what has become the world's song of friendly parting, "Auld Lang Syne."

From 1728 there was a regularly constituted Musical Society of Edinburgh, which from 1762 occupied St. Cecilia's Hall, modeled on the Parma Opera House. Besides hiring foreign instrumentalists and singers, its members, drawn from the leaders of society, took part in the orchestra and even supplied a composer of some charm, Thomas Erskine, sixth Earl of Kellie. Oddly enough, though Scots tunes were intruded into non-Scottish works, and though Continentals, like Haydn and Beethoven, used Scots themes, the musical Lord Kellie did not. There was a background for some decades in which one might have expected a national school of composition to arise, as later among the Czechs or Magyars; but nobody of sufficient genius arose in this field. Captain Topham, an Englishman, writing of Scotland in the 1770's, remarks on the extent to which music engrossed people: "In religion a Scotchman is grave and abstracted, in politics serious and deliberate: it is in the power of harmony alone to make him an enthusiast." But for creative purposes the enthusiasm achieved no more than songs and dance tunes; but here the harvest was rich. The violinist, or "fiddler," Niel Gow (1727–1807) had a lucrative business in collections of dance tunes, some of them by himself; his son Nathaniel Gow (1763–1831) was the ablest of four brothers, all composers as well as reputable executants. Burns and other poets continually had popular tunes in their heads to which to fit words; and the highest ranks shared the folk taste. Some of the best songs and ballads were written by aristocratic ladies: Lady Grizell Baillie, Lady Wardlaw, Lady Anne Lindsay, Miss Jean Elliot, Mrs. Alison Cockburn, and Lady Nairne, for example.

In poetry not attached to music, Scotland produced a poet who made an international impact, James Thomson (1700–48). The son of a Border minister, who died while exorcizing a ghost, he began publishing verses as a student at Edinburgh, and in 1725 set off, full of ambition, for London. A year later his poem *Winter* became famous almost overnight. It grew over the years into a multifarious digressive work, *The Seasons* (1730; finally revised in 1746), which greatly promoted the cult of the picturesque with its descriptions of nature. Storms of sand, as well as of thunder or snow, seascapes and landscapes, details about fauna and flora, numerous swatches of versification about the weather—all these elements freshened up the poetic atmosphere. Its influence was felt in Italy and France, and by Goethe later in the century. Thomson was apt, too, to load every rift with scientific lore, including the *avant-garde* ideas of Sir Isaac Newton.

Now and then there is a vivid flash, as when Thomson sees the remote geological age when

> *A shoreless ocean tumbled round the globe.*

Probably bird migrations by the Firth of Forth were in his mind's eye when he wrote the lines:

> *Infinite wings! till all the plume-dark air*
> *And white resounding shore are one wild cry.*

The projection of nature, and sentiment about nature, into poetry gave English literature a strong impetus towards the Romantic revival. On a more popular level, Thomson wrote the song "Rule, Britannia!" His plays have not held the stage, but his great literary success in London turned the thoughts of many a later Scots aspirant to that center. For generations gatherings of Scots writers toasted the Immortal Memory of Thomson, who had beaten the English in their own language, as later on Burns came to have his Immortal Memory celebrated annually.

The next Scots best seller in English was Tobias Smollett (1721–71), son of a laird near Loch Lomond. As an eighteen-year-old medical student he went to London, with a tragedy which nobody would print. Frustrated, he joined the Royal Navy as a surgeon, sailed to Jamaica, and married an heiress. A sentimental Jacobite, he commemorated the 1745 Rising with a poem, *The Tears of Scotland*. He had a turn also for scathing satires; but his most successful vein showed with a picaresque novel, *The Adventures of Roderick Random* (1748). Here for the first time the reader met the world of sailors, the British jack-tar, in an amalgam of farce and horse-play and down-to-earth medical observations that is like nothing earlier except Sir Thomas Urquhart's extended translation of Rabelais. From Continental tours Smollett used material for *The Adventures of Peregrine Pickle* (1751) and *Travels through France and Italy* (1766). He also did a vast deal of journalism and potboiling history. On return to Scotland in 1766 he was lionized, but he settled in Italy, at Leghorn, where he died in 1771. British sailors for genera-tions had the tradition of adorning his grave with laurel. Though a rancorous aristocrat in some ways, Smollett can put fairly the common man's viewpoint. In his last novel, *The Expedition of Humphrey Clinker*, his Scots soldier, Lismahagow, was perhaps the first fictional character to stir Scott and Galt to emulation by writing novels on Scot-tish themes.

In mid-century the essay was still the dominant literary form, and in this David Hume excelled. Like all Scots literati of his day, he had come under the influence of Addison and Steele and the *Spectator* tradition from London; but he was also steeped in Latin and Greek, being particularly fond of Lucian, and had spent some of his formative years in France. With most Scots writers one can assume a good early ground-ing in Latin, the staple of schooling in Edinburgh and all sizable towns; few had much Greek, but many had a fair reading ability in French. These factors mitigated the gen-eral Anglicizing influence of an English Bible and London prints. In conversation, Scots was almost universal until around 1800. Lacking means of hearing any sort of standard

English spoken extensively, Scots outside the higher courtier classes never learned to pronounce it as London society did. Thus Lord Pitfour, a judge, told a Scottish story to some English lawyers at Lincoln's Inn. They did not understand a word, and he complained, "I can utter no sound like an Englishman except sneezing." In the 1760's an attempt was made to get facilities for learning English systematically. In 1761 the Select Society hired an Irish actor, Thomas Sheridan, father of the playwright, to give courses for four weeks in St. Paul's Chapel, to three hundred gentlemen, paying a guinea each. He then gave a two weeks' course for ladies, perhaps assuming they were quicker in the uptake. In 1762, Edinburgh University hired the Rev. Dr. Hugh Blair as professor of Rhetoric and Belles-Lettres, the first academic chair of English literature in the world. Decades elapsed before any great proportion of Scots could speak English with facility. In general they were like Germans who could write French well enough, but were unready at talking it. William Craig, writing in *The Mirror*, an Edinburgh imitation of the London *Tatler*, confesses: "The *Scottish* dialect is our ordinary suit; the *English* is used only on solemn occasions. When a Scotsman therefore writes, he does it generally in trammels." "Jupiter" Carlyle records: "Since we began to affect speaking a foreign language, which the English dialect is to us, humour . . . is less apparent in conversation."

The effort to write with propriety in a quasi-foreign language tended to inhibit freedom of the creative imagination among eighteenth-century Scots, even had there not been other inhibiting factors, notably the practical and scientific and legalistic bent of most men's minds in that society. Therefore the innumerable essays of the period are, not astonishingly, seldom read today for bellettristic excellence of style. If they are read it is for their content. Hume's *Essays* survive by their masterly displays of high intelligence and wide learning over a wide range of topics, historical and sociological and economic, as well as as philosophical, in the narrower sense. But his contemporary reputation as a man of letters Hume owed chiefly to his *History of England* (1754–62). As a historian he pioneered in expounding social and economic developments and literary history. Concurrently William Robertson issued his *History of Scotland* (1759), and his *History of the Reign of Charles V* (1769). In the *Cambridge History of English Literature* one reads that British historical writing "was raised by Hume to a foremost place in our prose composition; its right to that place was maintained by Robertson.... That its two earliest reformers should both have been Scotsmen is one of the many illustrations of the activity of the Scots at that time in all the higher spheres of thought and of literary production."

In 1757, Hume wrote complacently: "Really it is admirable how many Men of Genius this Country produces at present. Is it not strange that, at a time when we have lost our Princes, our Parliaments, our independent Government, even the Presence of our chief Nobility, are unhappy, in our Accent & Pronunciation, speak a very corrupt Dialect of the Tongue which we make use of; is it not strange, I say, that, in these Circumstances we shou'd really be the People most distinguish'd for Literature in Europe?" Among those Hume had in mind was no doubt James Thomson; but also he thought of Home's *Douglas* tragedy, and the curious epic *The Epigoniad,* which earned the title of "The Scottish Homer" for William Wilkie, professor of Natural Philosophy at St. Andrews. There is frequently in smaller nations a tendency of patriots to exalt geese as swans, and Hume did that with Wilkie, claiming that his epic "is certainly a very singular Production, full of Sublimity & Genius, adorn'd by a noble, harmonious, forcible & even correct versification." Again, patriotism, aided by compassion, seems to have inspired Hume to praise the *Poems by Mr. Blacklock,* a blind minister, to whom Hume gave his salary as Keeper of the Advocates' Library.

Patriotism and history had been going hand in hand long enough in Scotland, since Barbour in the fourteenth century, and Boece and Buchanan in the sixteenth. In the early eighteenth century there was a growing movement to validate history from original documents, influenced, of course, by the work of Mabillon and the Bollandists in France. Thus James Anderson, W.S., issued in 1705, before the Union, *An Historical Essay, Shewing That the Crown and Kingdom of Scotland Is Imperial and Independent,* and in 1739, half a lifetime later, published *Selectus diplomatum et numismatum Scotiae thesaurus,* a critical source book, with an introduction by Thomas Ruddiman (1674–1757). Ruddiman was a general promoter of Scottish culture comparable, on a more academic level, to Allan Ramsay. Of a Jacobite background in Banffshire, he became assistant Keeper in the Advocates' Library (1702) and set about editing classics, like

Douglas' *Aeneid*, Drummond of Hawthornden's works, Abercromby's *Martial Achievements of the Scots Nation* (1711), and the works of Geoge Buchanan (1715), where he criticized adversely Buchanan's traducing of Mary Queen of Scots. He started in 1715 a printer's business, with his brother Walter, and in 1729 bought *The Caledonian Mercury* newspaper, run by his family until 1772. Thomas' son Thomas was gaoled in 1746 for running it as a Jacobite organ during the 1745 Rising; and died a year later from a disease contracted in Edinburgh's old prison, the Tolbooth. When the reformer John Howard visited it, for his report on the state of prisons (1784), he found it without ventilation, without drainage, with filth in every corner, and with one room where children were confined in air so foul that no visitor could risk entry. Poor convicts were kept in "a horrid cage," chained to an iron bar. One has to remember that judges passed this appalling den on their way home from the Parliament House to their cozy dinners with good claret and their studies full of elegantly bound volumes.

From the Roman Catholic side Thomas Innes, vice-principal of the Scots College at Paris, published *A Critical Essay on the Ancient Inhabitants of the Northern Parts of Britain, or Scotland*. Walter Goodall issued *A Brief Preface Concerning the First Planting of Christianity in Scotland* (1755), and other scholarly works. Even more rigorous in his attitude to sources was Sir David Dalrymple, Lord Hailes (1726–92), who worked on early Christian history and that of Scotland. Modeled on Hénault's *Chronological Abridgment of the History of France* (1768), Hailes's *Annals* of Scotland set a

new standard for critical history. That for some of these Scots
Latin was felt as still an international language is exemplified
in Hailes's Latin version of Hume's autobiography (1787).
He also prepared *A Specimen of a Glossary of the Scottish
Language*. English was, however, increasingly felt to be a
new international medium, and Hume persuaded Edward
Gibbon to write his *Decline and Fall* in English, Gibbon
having contemplated French. Hume wrote: "Let the French
. . . triumph in the present diffusion of their tongue. Our
solid and increasing establishments in America, where we
need less dread the inundation of Barbarians, promise a
superior stability and duration to the English language."

An unexpected injection of fresh poetic inspiration into
English occurred in 1760, with the publication of *Fragments
of Ancient Poetry Collected in the Highlands of Scotland,
and Translated from the Gaelic or Erse Language*. The so-
called translator was James Macpherson (1736–96), a poor
young man from a family of chieftains in Inverness-shire,
educated at the two universities of Aberdeen. He was on the
Borders as tutor to the future Lord Lynedoch, a famous general to be, when he met John Home, author of *Douglas*.
Highland regiments had been conspicuous in the conquests
of Canada and India, and Home was eager to know about
the Celts and their poetry. Macpherson showed him a version
of a poem on *The Death of Oscar*, and other pieces, which
Home handed on to the Rev. Dr. Hugh Blair, of Edinburgh,
an eminent preacher and critic. The Faculty of Advocates
subscribed funds to send Macpherson round the Highlands
and Isles, where ministers and lairds showed him sundry old

parchment manuscripts, and reciters dictated to him masses
of Gaelic verses. From such materials Macpherson concocted
his purported translations. Lord Bute, the Prime Minister,
summoned him to London, where he issued, in 1762, *Fingal:
An Ancient Epic Poem in Six Books*. He alleged that some
Highland gentlemen had aided him in completing the epic
poem, and, "It is only my business to lay it before the reader,
as I have found it." He followed up *Fingal* with an eight-
book epic, *Temora* (1763). Blair found them all "noble . . .
magnificent . . . amazing . . . sublime." Their influence ran
throughout Europe. Bygone kings and heroes warring amid
twilit mists and rocks and torrents somehow appealed to the
overfed denizens of gilded drawing rooms. Macpherson in
fact owed something to Homer and Virgil and to the King
James version of the Psalms and Isaiah, as well as to Irish
or Scots Gaelic poems and tales; and a good deal to his own
inventiveness. His "Celtic twilight" misrepresents the typical
Gaelic poetry, which is vivid, muscular, and rapid; but it had
a fantastic vogue, greatly aided by political partisanship.
Skeptics demanded to see the originals; and Macpherson
supplied some Gaelic manuscripts to his London publishers,
Beckett and De Hondt, who advertised that they would print
them if subscribers came forward. English critics, ignorant
of Gaelic, denounced the epics as shameless forgeries but did
not examine the manuscripts. Had they done so, doubtless
they would have found that Macpherson had mixed old elements at his discretion and added as the spirit moved him.
Late in life he translated his purported translations into a
Gaelic that had become somewhat rusty with him, and most

of his Gaelic *Ossian* got into print eventually (1807). Meantime Macpherson had made a political career, becoming an M.P., and being honored with burial in Westminster Abbey. He had also made money, including £3,000 for his *History of Great Britain from 1660 to 1714* (1775), where he used documents to expose the intrigues of leading Whig magnates with the exiled Stuarts in France. He was a Tory, like Hume, whose revisions of his own *History of England* inclined towards a more favorable view of the Tories at over one hundred places.

"Ossian" Macpherson's vogue has not lasted, but readers today relish more than ever the works of James Boswell (1740–95), which were little valued in his own time. He wrote a novel, *Dorando* (1767), about the litigation concerning the estates of the Duke of Douglas, which roused keen passions in Scotland. He wrote an *Account of Corsica* (1768), manifesting the vicarious nationalism frequently found in Scots, crusading for the freedom of other peoples. In 1773 he served as bear leader to Samuel Johnson round the Highlands, and described their tour (1785) and Johnson's life (1791). But even greater fame has accrued recently from opportune finds of Boswelliana in remote country houses.

Another Ayrshireman, Robert Burns (1759–96), first attained celebrity locally with satires on local ecclesiastical politics, prompted in part by his having personally fallen foul of the parish minister and ruling elders, through extramarital relations with his future wife and others. As English was the language of religion, Burns's revolt against the "Unco Guid" found vent in colloquial Scots. His constant propensity to fall in love inspired him to song, as well as satire; and he hit on the idea of issuing a printed volume of his work to pay his passage to the West Indies, where he planned to manage a sugar plantation. His trunk was on the way to the port of Greenock when he heard that his *Poems Chiefly in the Scottish Dialect* (1786) had been praised by leading critics in the capital. He went there and was lionized. Himself the son of a poor tenant farmer, and the spokesman of the French revolutionary ideas of liberty, equality, and fraternity, he could yet associate on terms of friendship with judges and professors and duchesses and lairds. The most exclusive sodality in Edinburgh, the Royal Company of Archers, founded in 1676 as the royal bodyguard for Scotland, made him a member. The gentlemen of the Caledonian Hunt subscribed for a new edition of his poems. At a meeting of Freemasons he was hailed as "Caledonia's Bard, brother Burns!" Himself deriving from the tradition of metropolitan sophisticated utterance in Scots verse, carried on by Allan Ramsay and Robert Fergusson—on whose grave Burns erected a headstone—Burns gave a new impetus to the use of Scots for verse, in lyrics, satire, comic narrative, and discursive epistle; and this new impetus was a factor in Walter Scott's use of the tongue in his novels. The democratic content of his poems influenced the Romantic movement in England and elsewhere, and, through translations, continues still today to influence poets as far afield as Russia and Hungary.

Scott's influence has been equally wide, above all through his creation of the historical novel. The Edinburgh background of literary traditions partly explains how he came to this important innovation; but there are also personal factors that suggest both how he came to it and how late. His father, Walter Scott, W.S., was a grave lawyer, fond of legal lore, Calvinist theology, the Latin language, and the playing of golf and the violincello. He had married Anne Rutherford, daughter of a medical professor. Both were of ancient families, and lived in comfortable circumstances, with many acquaintances in fashionable society. In early boyhood the young Walter was partly crippled in his right leg, by infantile paralysis, and reacted valiantly against it, like Franklin D. Roosevelt later. He was sent to recuperate at his grandfather's Border sheep farm, where he imbibed local lore from the ewe-milkers and the *cow-bailie*. Until death he always had a Border burr in his deep, strong voice. But he also spent a year, around the age of five, at Bath, the most fashionable health resort in England; and there he learned how the best English society pronounced their language and behaved themselves. Thus Scott had the advantage of contrasting and appreciating the two languages, even more thoroughly than Allan Ramsay with his mixed Anglo-Scots parentage. When Scott came to write novels it was natural for him to use standard English for the narrative and reflective parts, but to use a rich and copious Scots for his Scottish characters, especially the rustic and old-fashioned types. His formal education was desultory, being interrupted by ill health. At the High School of Edinburgh he got a good reading knowledge of Latin, and elsewhere picked up for himself Italian, Spanish, and German. He did little in Greek. When he spoke French it was full of medievalisms. Among books that early impressed him were Pope's translation of Homer, Ramsay's *Ever Green,* Macpherson's Ossianic material, Spenser, Percy's *Reliques,* and a version of Tasso; but his omnivorous reading included Richardson, Fielding, Smollett, and other novelists, including Henry Mackenzie, whose sentimental masterpiece, *The Man of Feeling,* impressed Burns so profoundly that he wore out two copies of it. At Edinburgh University, Scott's studies were superficial, and interrupted by illness. When aged about fifteen he began an apprenticeship in his father's law firm, displaying an astonishing capacity for work. Once he wrote out 120 folio pages, with no interval for food or rest, to earn money for the theater and to borrow books from a circulating library. Possibly through overwork, he had a long illness, but by the age of nineteen had become robust, tall, and muscular, able, in spite of his deformed leg, to walk thirty miles a day over rough country. Having decided to become an advocate, he went to classes in Roman law and Scots law, the latter taught by David Hume's nephew; and joined the faculty in 1792. He went much into fashionable society, his closest friend being William Clerk of Penicuik; his thesis for admission, on the disposal of the corpses of criminals, was dedicated to the leading judge, Lord Braxfield, a neighbor in George's Square. In the political agitations of the 1790's, Scott became hotheadedly Tory. For example, in April, 1794, when Irish medical students called for French revolutionary songs in the theater, Scott led the young Tory Advocates in a battle with cudgels, shillelaghs, and made the Irish sing "God Save the King." He took the lead in forming a body of vounteer cavalry, in 1797, becoming quartermaster and secretary. Cockburn says it became with Scott "an absolute passion, indulgence in which gratified his feudal taste for war and his jovial sociableness." He was particularly fierce at the exercise of slashing with a sabre at a turnip set on a pole, to represent a French soldier. At the end of 1797 he married a refugee French lady, Charlotte Charpentier, with whom he had fallen in love at first sight, when seeing her out riding near Carlisle. A month before the marriage he wrote to her: "I do not like to leave the Cavalry tho' attended with some expence because my situation in the Corps gives me access to the Duke of Buccleugh & several other persons who may be useful to me." It is important to remember the clannish context in which Scotsmen of that age had to pursue their careers, and also the desire for money that directed so much of Scott's literary activity.

As a boy Scott had been collecting ballads, many of which he got by heart without trying; and as a young advocate he made several trips into Liddesdale, the wildest part of the Borders, with Robert Shortreed, sheriff-substitute of Roxburghshire. But his first venture as an author was a verse translation of a German ballad, Bürger's *Lenore,* written for Miss Cranstoun, afterwards Gräfin Purgstall. She had copies elegantly printed for him to present to the lady on whose affections he had then set his heart, Miss Williamina Stuart Belshes of Invermay; but she married in 1793 a rich baronet, Sir William Forbes. Scott's copy of Bürger had been secured for him by a German countess, Gräfin Brühl, who had married Scott of Harden, the chief of Scott's branch of the clan; she had been daughter of an ambassador in London, and was the first lady of high international fashion to take him up. She went carefully through his verses, correcting away Scotticisms and rhymes where he had given a Scots pronunciation to a word common to both Scots and English. His dilettante literary interests, while he tried to build up a practice at the Bar, were rather in history than in poetry; but the precipitate marriage, and the need to find money, led to more versification. By chance, Scott met "Monk" Lewis, novelist and M.P., the reigning arbiter of literary fashion in London, who invited him to contribute to a miscellany he was preparing, and arranged for a London publisher to issue a translation of Goethe's *Götz von Berlichingen*. Scott took his wife to London to celebrate, and met many in literary society there. In 1799, through the Duke of Buccleugh's interest with Henry Dundas, Scott was made sheriff of Selkirkshire, which gave him a secure income for life, for duties not too arduous. Thus professionally anchored, part-time, to his ancestral Borders, Scott resumed the collection of ballads, and in 1802 issued two volumes of his *Minstrelsy of the Scottish Border*. In editing them Scott was sometimes moved to add, and the vein of original composition proved productive. In 1805 he issued *The Lay of the Last Minstrel,* an instant and lucrative success, to be followed by *Marmion* and *The Lady of the Lake,* containing several Ossianic swatches. These poems brought in thousands of guineas, and he set about building a baronial castle on the Tweed, Abbotsford (1811); to enlarge the estate around it more guineas were needed. At the same time the vogue of Byron's poems was causing a fall-off in the demand for Scott's. Scott had already in 1805 written some chapters of a novel about Scotland during the 1745 Rising, and he now completed it, to issue it anonymously as *Waverley* (1814). It was astutely dedicated to Henry Mackenzie as "the Scottish Addison"; and the anonymity may have been in part to secure publicity by mystification. It was an immediate success. Cockburn wrote: "The unexpected newness of the thing, the profusion of original characters, the Scotch language, Scotch scenery, Scotch men and women, the simplicity of the writing, and the graphic force of the descriptions, all struck us with an electric shock of delight." Much of the material came from personal acquaintance with such men as the veteran Jacobite, Stewart of Invernahyle, a client of Scott's father, One of the literary influences was Maria Edgeworth, with her "regional" novels about the Irish country gentry. After *Waverley*, Scott published some more poems, notably *The Lord of the Isles* (1815), but mainly exploited his new talent as novelist, with *Guy Mannering, The Antiquary, Old Mortality, Rob Roy*, and *The Heart of Midlothian* (1815–19). During a serious illness he was dosed with opium, and dictated *The Bride of Lammermoor* (1819) in a semiconscious state. Later, says his printer James Ballantyne, "he did not recollect one single incident, character, or conversation it contained." Yet, like even his feeblest works, it has many vivid and dramatic passages and moments; it became the basis for the opera *Lucia di Lammermoor*. *Quentin Durward* (1823), about a Scotsman in the French king's Guard, increased Scott's European reputation; and the publisher Constable reported in 1822 that, when *The Fortunes of Nigel* came out, "I actually saw them reading it in the Streets as they passed along. I assure you there is no exaggeration in this. A new novel from the Author of Waverley puts aside in other words puts down for the time every other literary performance." After the general financial crash of 1825–26 had brought down Constable, Scott, and the Ballantynes, his printers, together, Scott set to work, with honorable determination, to write enough to pay off his creditors. In two years his trustees made some £40,000 from his productions. The astonishing thing is that, even among the weakest of the later potboilers, Scott retains the faculty to re-create the past vividly, with a genial width of human sympathy and plenty of engaging characters. No writer before him so well portrayed the common people. The fault of most of his novels is in the insipidity and shallowness of his heroes and heroines, perhaps due to a certain gentlemanly reticence about intruding too deeply into the secrets of the individual's conduct, and to Scott's early trauma in his pursuit of Miss Stuart Belshes. But innumerable historical characters are brought to life again, as are countless imaginary minor personalities. In plots and narrative style Scott is incredibly careless; but his dialogue, especially when in Scots, is wonderfully lively. In creating the historical novel, he gave a new dimension to the writing of history.

While writing largely for guineas, which the English could contribute more abundantly than the Scots, and therefore addressing primarily the "gentle reader," that is to say the upper-class English and Scots, Scott contributed powerfully, as had Burns, to the survival of the sense of nationality among the Scots, and to the continued use of the Scots tongue for literature. But by restricting it to dialogue, and especially to rustic, lower-class, and old-fashioned characters, he tended to relegate it to the status of a patois, a regional dialect, no longer capable of dealing with all the themes of literature. His contemporary John Galt (1779–1839) took a rather different line in his Scottish novels, like *The Annals of the Parish* (1821), first drafted in 1813, before Scott's *Waverley* appeared. Galt freely mixed Scots words, idioms, and speech-rhythms into his narrative and reflective passages in English; but even he never attempted to write a whole novel entirely in Scots prose. No publisher would have risked capital to issue it, whereas the Anglo-Scots compromise was commercially a wonderful proposition, for a time at least.

There was, however, in Scotland a nationwide response to Dr. John Jamieson's *Etymological Dictionary of the Scottish Language*, originally issued in 1808, under royal patronage, with a *Supplement* in 1825, to which innumerable individuals had sent data. In the Gaelic tongue, too, wide interest was taken, partly religious, with new work on translating the Bible, and partly literary. Duncan Ban Macintyre (1724–1812), an Argyll gamekeeper who in later life had a sinecure in the Edinburgh City Guard, sold three editions of his poems during his lifetime (1768; 1790; 1804). The greatest Gaelic poet, Alasdair MacMhaighstir Alasdair (1700–70), published at Edinburgh in 1751 a collection of his poems, only to have many copies of them burned by the hangman; he had been a militant Jacobite. In 1741 he had made the first Scots Gaelic dictionary, for the Society in Scotland for Propagating Christian Knowledge; but they later dismissed him for the indelicacy of his own compositions. Dugald Buchanan (1716–68), a fine hymn-writer, printed his *Spiritual Hymns* in Edinburgh, in 1767, while attending the University. To this age belong also the Gaelic satirists John MacCodrum (1693–1779) and Rob Donn Mackay (1714–78), and William Ross (1762–90), author of love lyrics and pastoral poems: many of their pieces were orally current among the Gaelic speakers of Edinburgh, who were numerous among the officers, soldiers, and domestic servants.

The main stream of Edinburgh literary activity, however, lay not in novels or poems, Scots or Gaelic, but in expository prose in English, such as that of Adam Smith (1723–90), and the contributors to the original *Encyclopaedia Britannica* (1771), the periodicals called *The Mirror* and *The Lounger*, and, most influential of all, *The Edinburgh Review* (1802–1929). Adam Smith was born in Kirkcaldy, across the Forth from Edinburgh, and schooled at the universities of Glasgow and Oxford; he gave lectures in Edinburgh shortly before 1750 on English literature and style. Later he censured Samuel Johnson for admitting too many low and improper words into his English dictionary. He became a professor at Glasgow in 1751, selling his chair in 1764 to become traveling tutor to the young Duke of Buccleugh, at a salary of £300 a year, the same as Hume got for tutoring a young Lord Annandale; but Smith got the same sum as a pension for the rest of his life. It was to his *Theory of Moral Sentiments* (1759) that Smith owed his European reputation, and the job with the Duke. While traveling, he got bored during a stay at Toulouse, and began his more momentous work, *The Wealth of Nations*. Settling in his native Kirkcaldy, Smith worked for six years on the book, frequently visiting Hume, who kept a room for him in his house. After publication in 1776, Smith became commissioner of customs in Scotland, and marched daily to his office, holding a cane on his right shoulder like a soldier his musket. Smith was a disciplined thinker and writer. His basic doctrine is theological, that there is a divinely pre-established harmony in human affairs between the maximum happiness of mankind and the efforts of each individual human being acting freely. Here Smith follows Frances Hutcheson; but in the economic applications of the doctrine he is largely reflecting the experience of Glasgow merchants in his time, and reacting against the mercantilist state-controlled systems in vogue, especially in France. Hume's commercial essays were also formative for Smith. There is no doubt that the doctrine of Free Trade was salutary for Scotland in her political submersion in the United Kingdom dominated by English and London-centered interests; if the nation was not to have its own national government, then the less government it had of any sort the better, so that individual Scots and groups of them could get ahead with running their own farms, banks, factories, shipping lines, and so forth, without foreign control; and for the larger part of the period from 1776 to 1914, Smith's views became in fact the dominant practice in Britain.

Adam Smith's chair for most of his time was that of Moral Philosophy, and the parallel chair in Edinburgh must be reckoned one of the chief influences in the Edinburgh type of civilization. Consider, for instance, Adam Ferguson (1723–1815), professor of Moral Philosophy from 1764 to 1785. Son of a Perthshire minister, he talked Gaelic, and Whiggery in Gaelic; but would sing Jacobite songs, once the danger of a Jacobite succession was past. Offered a chaplaincy in the Black Watch by the Duchess of Atholl, he took part in the battle of Fontenoy, broadsword in hand, at the head of the column. When the colonel told him his commission did not entitle him to such an activity, Ferguson cried, "Damn my commission!" and flung it at the colonel. His sermons were merely ethical essays, abounding with citations from Plato and Aristotle, as well as denunciations of the Pope and the Pretender. Soon after resigning his chaplaincy, he became tutor to the sons of Lord Bute, and in 1759, professor of Natural Philosophy, about which he knew nothing. After five years he exchanged that for Moral Philosophy, which included political economy, literary criticism, and psychology. His first publication thereafter was an *Essay on the History of Civil Society* (1765). His chair did not hinder his traveling as tutor to the Earl of Chesterfield, and visiting Voltaire. He commented on this: "Had I not been in the Highlands of Scotland, I might be of their mind who think the inhabitants of Paris and Versailles the only polite people in the world." In 1776 he went to America, as secretary to the British Commissioners negotiating with George Washington and the Congress. Interested in republicanism, he worked on his *History of the Roman Republic* (1783), a set of lectures on politics, with a marked Stoic bias. It was in his house that the boy Scott met the poet Burns. In 1793 he set off, with a single servant, to Italy, in the midst of war, to satisfy his curiosity about some matters for a new edition of his history. He lived a vegetarian and teetotaler, to his ninety-third year, occasionally visiting his relative, the scientist Joseph Black. His son Sir Adam Ferguson, Scott's friend, tells how the veteran philosophers " rioted together" over a boiled turnip.

Ferguson's successor, Dugald Stewart (1753–1828), was son of a professor of mathematics, and educated at the universities of Edinburgh and Glasgow. At the age of nineteen he ran the mathematics classes for his father, when ill, and took on also the work of Ferguson's chair when he was in America, adding to that a course on astronomy. This encyclopedic versatility is the hallmark of the Scots intellectual of this age. From 1785 to 1820, Stewart held the Moral Philosophy chair, doing the work himself until 1810. Cockburn calls his class "the great era in the progress of young men's minds." Stewart, he said, "exalted all his powers by certain other qualifications. . . . an unimpeachable personal character, devotion to the science he taught, an exquisite taste, an imagination imbued with poetry and oratory, liberality of opinion, and the loftiest morality."

Very different was Stewart's successor, John Wilson (1785–1852), son of a wealthy family from Paisley, and educated at the universities of Glasgow and Oxford, where he won the Newdigate prize for poetry. He was more distinguished for athletic prowess and boundless animal vitality. He married an English heiress and lived in the Cumberland Lake district, enjoying country life and the scribbling of verses. In

1814 he joined the Faculty of Advocates, and in 1817 became joint editor of *Blackwood's Magazine,* the Tory literary organ designed to fire back at the Whiggish and Radical *Edinburgh Review* of 1802. His appointment to the Moral Philosophy chair was a Tory political job of a fairly outrageous sort. The Town Council elected him by 21 votes to 9 against Sir William Hamilton, at that time the best philosopher in Britain, and later his colleague as professor of Logic. As Scott wrote to his future son-in-law John Gibson Lockhart, the Tory government could give "only a tacit and underhand support." Thomas Carlyle recorded "how hugely ill it was taken by the vast majority of talking and newspapering mankind." But Scott a year later was happy to assure the second Lord Melville, Harry Dundas' son, that Wilson's class "is throngd to the very door & he has pocketed already £700 of fees. The lectures are splendidly eloquent." Scott goes on to add: "I have been chosen President of the Royal Society here which keeps one feather out of a Whig bonnet." This is a reminder how much the literary activity of the time was a *littérature engagée.* John Wilson's pseudonym, Christopher North, became famous in Scotland, and wherever *Blackwood's Magazine* was read, in England and Ireland, India and America. Incidentally, it came out in April, 1817, at two shillings and sixpence, and still appears at the same price in 1965, a record for stability.

Considering together Ferguson, Stewart, and Wilson, one has the impression that students found in the Edinburgh Professor of Moral Philosophy primarily a man of the world who could alert them to a variety of current opinions on matters philosophical and literary, and give them a training in public speaking and the art of writing essays. Most of the students in the class were around fifteen or sixteen, and the custom was for the professor to do a good deal of tutorial work with them. Holders of the chair of Logic applied a similar technique, as did the professors of Humanity (Latin) and Greek. The finer skills of classical scholarship, such as writing Greek verses, were hardly cultivated; and Latin poetry had been neglected, though from 1550 to 1700, Scotland had been eminent in it. Dr. Johnson allowed that "The Latin poetry of *Deliciae Poetarum Scotorum* [the anthology of 1637] would have done honour to any nation," though written when, as he thought, "their tables were coarse as the feasts of Eskimeaux, and their houses filthy as the cottages of Hottentots." The Scottish universities did little for the classics until reforms in the Indian and British civil services made it necessary for ambitious Scots to compete with men from English schools and the universities of Oxford and Cambridge which specialized in Latin and Greek. In Scott's age the Edinburgh Faculty of Arts offered rather something more like the general studies program of an American liberal arts college nowadays; and apparently that is what the students and their parents desired, for they crowded out John Wilson's classroom. As the bulk of a professor's income came from their fees, payment was in effect by results. In 1821, Wilson's £700 would be equivalent to the year's earnings of about thirty farm-servants or twenty-four masons. In return his course would be useful to intending ministers or lawyers, and those hardy all-purpose managerial Scots who played so large a part in running banks, insurance companies, and large public or private enterprises in London or the overseas portions of the English-speaking world.

The practical and versatile trend is seen notably in the first *Encyclopaedia Britannica*, published in three volumes at Edinburgh in 1771. It is subtitled "A Dictionary of Arts & Sciences Compiled upon a New Plan, in Which the Different Sciences & Arts Are Digested into Distinct Treatises or Systems. By a Society of Gentlemen in Scotland." These were James Tytler, Colin Macfarquhar, and William Smellie. It was illustrated by 160 copperplates, by Andrew Bell. Studying the volumes, one has the impression that the *Encyclopaedia* was just the thing for a serious-minded Scots laird, intent on unified resource development on a family estate, with its comparatively full articles on such topics as agriculture, architecture, arithmetic, bleaching, chemistry, commerce, exchange, fortification, gardening, horsemanship, law, logic, mechanics, medicine, moral philosophy, metaphysics, midwifery, musick, navigation, shorthand writing, surgery, trigonometry, and watch and clock work. By contrast words are not wasted on such a topic as sin, described as "a breach or transgression of some divine law, or command." In 1777 a revised edition came out, and the publication became an Edinburgh institution. After the defeat of Napoleon, Archibald Constable, whom Scott called "The Napoleon of Publishers," relaunched it on a much greater scale, edited by Macvey Napier, with contributions from leading authorities all over the world (1816).

Archibald Constable, as publisher, made possible the astonishing impact of the *Edinburgh Review* from 1802. Starting with a printing of 750 copies, as a quarterly at five shillings, it got to 13,000 copies an issue, with frequent reprintings of back numbers. At the same period the *Times* newspaper of London had a circulation of 8,000. The venture was launched by three young men in their twenties, advocates with time on their hands in the Parliament House, at the suggestion of an English clergyman, the Whig wag Sydney Smith, who had been in Edinburgh since 1798 as tutor to a rich young Englishman. Smith wrote of the city: "I like this place extremely and cannot help thinking that for a literary man, by which term I mean a man who is fond of Letters, it is the most eligible situation in the island. It unites good Libraries liberally managed, learned men without any other system than that of pursuing truth, very good general society, large healthy virgins, with mild pleasing countenances and white swelling breasts—shores washed by the Sea—the romantic grandeur of antient and the beautiful regularity of modern, building, and boundless floods of oxygen." The three young advocates were Frances Jeffrey, who became sole editor in 1803, Francis Horner, and Henry Brougham. Horner, son of an Edinburgh merchant, and grandson of a Writer to the Signet, had been dux boy of the High School, and was to become a financial expert of the House of Commons, before his early death. Brougham, half-English, was a grandnephew of the historian Robertson; after early distinction in science, he busied himself mainly with law and reform, becoming Lord Chancellor. Jeffrey, grandson of an Edinburgh barber, and son of an official in the law courts, had studied in the universities of Glasgow, Oxford, and Edinburgh, and became, as Macaulay wrote, "more nearly an universal genius than any man of our time." Madame de Stael wrote of his *Review* in 1815: "If some being from another climate were to come to this and desire to know in what work the highest pitch of human intellect might be found, he ought to be shown the *Edinburgh Review*." Emerson recorded: "Like most young men at that time, I was much indebted to the men of Edinburgh and of the *Edinburgh Review*." Yet Jeffrey exerted this world-wide influence in his spare time from a busy legal career, ending as a reforming Lord Advocate and a judge.

The first issue came out in October, 1802, during a short peace in the Napoleonic wars. Its subtitle was *Critical Journal*, and it bore the motto, "Judex damnatur cum nocens absolvitur," "The judge is condemned when the guilty is acquitted." Smith had proposed the frivolous "Musam tenui meditamur avena," paraphrased as "We cultivate literature on a little oatmeal." Wit and flippancy were never wanting, but the balance of the *Review* was always judicial and critical. Cockburn remembered the effect of the new periodical as electrical. "It was an entire and instant change of everything that the public had been accustomed to in that sort of composition." Instead of reviews abstracting and puffing what booksellers wished to sell, here were independent gentlemen expounding and criticizing, often at great length, books selected by them as important. Constable gave Jeffrey a free hand as editor; and, after some issues written for nothing, paid Jeffrey £200 a year for editing, and paid reviewers a minimum of ten guineas for a sheet (sixteen printed pages). Anonymity was the rule, which helped publicity by guessing authorship. It also made Jeffrey as editor liable to challenges to duels, as by the Irish poet Tom Moore, an encounter inter-rupted by the police. (They later became firm friends.) Jeffrey was a small man, little over five feet tall, but of bound-less energy and liveliness, amorous, gay, and kindhearted, though never free from pessimism. In editing over the years he inculcated the view that happiness depends on kindness and the performance of duties; in reviewing he always kept in mind the moral bearing of an author's personality and tenets.

The first number, of 252 pages, starts with a review of a book by J. J. Mounier, exiled president of the first French National Assembly, on the influence attributed to philoso-phers, Freemasons, and Illuminati in the French Revolution. It goes on with a witty notice of a sermon by the Rev. Dr. Samuel Parr, largely aimed at William Godwin, Shelley's father-in-law, and another of Godwin's reply. There are many pages about travels in India, Turkey, Egypt, North America, and a piece about the causes of emigration from the Highlands and Islands of Scotland. There follows a review of Robert Southey's metrical romance *Thalaba*, a product of the Lake School of poetry with its "affectation of great simplicity and familiarity of language." The reviewer states: "Now, this style, we conceive, possesses no one char-acter of excellence; it is feeble, low, and disjointed; without elegance, and without dignity; the offspring, we should im-agine, of mere indolence and neglect, or the unhappy fruit of a system that would teach us to undervalue that vigilance and labour which sustained the loftiness of Milton, and gave energy and direction to the pointed and fine propriety of Pope." But the *Review* is not primarily concerned with poetry and imaginative writing. Much of its concern is with finance, with thirty pages on the paper credit of Great Britain; or with science, as Playfair's *Illustrations of the Huttonian Theory*; or with politics, notably the French naval threat to the sugar colonies in the West Indies; or with sermons, or medicine, or the state of Scottish schools. Subsequent comment has largely touched on the *Review's* strictures on the Romantic poets; but its historical importance lies far more in its influence in economics and politics and the promotion of a public-spirited enlightened opinion about the reform of abuses in all fields. Though issued in the blue and buff cover that showed Whig principles, it did not start as a party political organ, and it had Tories like Scott and Wilberforce among its early contributors. After a few years it became more partisan, and helped to turn Whiggery from a narrow aristocratic cousinhood into a party with a substantial middle-class backing. In response the Tories promoted the *Quarterly Review* (1808), issued by the London Scots publisher John Murray, and *Blackwood's Magazine* (1817), in Edinburgh itself. This was marked by a raffish and rough tone of gross personal attacks. Robert Mudie (1777–1842), in *The Modern Athens* (1825), comments that its writers "affected to be adepts in debauchery, and pretended to keep no secrets from their readers, even in the most unseemly of their carousals." He is here referring to the *Noctes Ambrosianae*, a series of

139

scenes in Ambrose's tavern near the Register House. Of this series of "jovial dramatic fiction," mainly by John Wilson, alias Christopher North, Cockburn writes: "There is not so curious and original a work in the English or Scotch languages. It is a most singular and delightful outpouring of criticism, politics, and descriptions of feeling, character, and scenery, of verse and prose, and maudlin eloquence, and especially of wild fun. It breathes the very essence of the Bacchanalian revel of clever men. And its Scotch is the best Scotch that has been written in modern times. I am really sorry for the poor one-tongued Englishman."

Ninety per cent of this Scoto-Anglic dramatic outpouring came from a Professor of Moral Philosophy, appointed by a Tory political job. In fact the tavern, or "public house," as it was called by a recent fashion, had all along been the main focus of Scottish education, as a lifelong experience. The two thousand or so students of the University were not housed in colleges, but lived with their families or in lodgings. As a major tourist center, Edinburgh had become abundantly supplied with excellent hotels, and many families leased rooms to students, or to law clerks from all over Scotland, serving apprenticeships in the legal capital. Mudie, who had taught in Inverness Academy and Dundee High School, remarked that Edinburgh education "is chiefly taken up with removing the restraints that have been imposed in other places, and by other systems,"and he found "no place where manners and morals of young persons are so free." He found the Edinburgh youth of the 1820's to be "showy and jovial as companions, not very pre-eminent for sagacity as counsellors, or trust-worthiness as friends." Worse, he reported that "there is perhaps no city in which vice is more generally or more obtrusively practiced, than in this self-boasted model of taste and purity." Jokes current in Parliament House had a broadness which would not be tolerated in similar places elsewhere. "The broad and vulgar debaucheries" of Edinburgh people "not only occupy more of their time, but engross much more of their conversation, than is the case in the British metropolis." Mudie comments, too, on the brothels frequented by the "dashing bloods," that "the squalor of a house is no objection whatever. Scotch economy prompts them to get everything cheap, and hence there are in the Athens [i.e., Edinburgh] sinks of vice, supported and frequented by those who call themselves gentlemen, that would hardly be tolerated, or even supposed, in the very lowest neighborhood of any other place." The practice of drinking Mudie found to be habitual and deep, and he noted they were "democrats in their drink." It was an Edinburgh maxim that "the bottle raises or lowers all people to the same level." A judge having disappeared for three days, when required for an important case, was eventually found on the tower of St. Giles, drinking and playing cards with two or three caddies, or street messengers.

Within a few years of Mudie's strictures the new Puritan movement, which culminated in the forming of the Free Church in 1843, did something to abate or hide the drunkenness and debauchery of which he complains; and in that movement Jeffrey's *Edinburgh Review* tended to aid, whereas *Blackwood's Magazine* appealed initially rather to the

141

unreformed. Pressure to conform and the lust for self-grati-
fication led to some odd manifestations of hypocrisy or
double personality: notably in Deacon William Brodie, a
respectable merchant by day and an astute burglar by night.
He was hanged (1788) on a gibbet of his own design. Deacon
Brodie's case gave a hint to Robert Louis Stevenson, the
creator of Dr. Jekyll and Mr. Hyde. Mudie asserted that "the
people of consideration, and not the populace," were "the
most religiously irreligious people that one can imagine. A
few years ago, when it was the fashion to be sceptical, the
very name of going to church stamped a man as belonging
to the veriest vulgar; but the kirk has again come into vogue,
and it is now just as much a mark of vulgarity not to go
there, as it then was to go. . . . the official men find their interest in being kirk-elders; ladies and gentlemen see each
other; and after so pious and praise-worthy a thing as church-
going, there can be little harm in an assignation, or an ad-
journment to a tavern-dinner. . . . When you have witnessed
the deep and prolonged potations of some Athenian worthy
upon the Saturday night, when you have heard the racy
jokes and anecdotes with which he enlivened his cups, and
when you have marked how small store he set by the principles as well as the practices of religion, you wonder at the
calm face that he puts on as he stands at the church-door,
watching the pence and sixpences that are thrown into the
charity-plate. It is all a cloak, however."

There were even some believers in a certain form of popular
Calvinism who thought that God's few elect were licensed,
and indeed foreordained, to commit whatever evil they

pleased. In 1824, James Hogg, "the Ettrick Shepherd" (1770–1835), published, anonymously, his novel *The Private Memoirs and Confessions of a Justified Sinner*, in which he presents such a character. It could have been a historical novel, not a work wholly of creative imagination. Conversely, Lord Byron (1788–1826), who described himself as "half a Scot by birth, and bred a whole one," believed himself to be predestined to damnation. He wrote to his future wife: "I was bred in Scotland among Calvinists in the first part of my life"; and Lady Byron later testified that Byron "had the gloomiest Calvinistic tenets. . . . I, like all connected with him, was broken against the rock of predestination." He had them from his mother, Catherine Gordon; from his Aberdonian nurse, Agnes Gray; and from his rigid Presbyterian tutor, Paterson. He believed his congenital clubfootedness to be just another proof of his predestined damnation, and this conviction may have led him to indulge the basest sexual propensities, on the principle that one might as well be hanged for a sheep as a lamb. George Finlay, the Scots historian of Greece, wrote about his talks with Byron: "Both his character and conduct presented unceasing contradictions. It seemed as if two different souls occupied his body alternately." Byron makes a similar comment on Burns: "What an antithetical mind!—tenderness, roughness,—delicacy, coarseness—sentiment, sensuality—soaring and grovelling, dirt and deity—all mixed up in that one compound of inspired clay!"

What Byron found true of Burns seems largely applicable to Scott's Edinburgh—both his Edinburghs.

7

Castes and Fashions

THOUGH IN SCOTT'S TIME the classes of Edinburgh society mingled as a rule in a friendly and familiar way, still there was marked class consciousness at all levels. In *The Autobiography of a Working Man*, Somerville complains that "The masons were intolerable tyrants to their labourers." In contrast Lord Provost Creech laments the high wages and indiscipline of journeymen in the 1790's: "Many of them riot on Sunday, are idle all Monday, and can afford to do this on five days labour." Maidservants, with three or four pounds of wages a year, "dress as fine as their mistresses."

At the top of the social tree were, of course, the Scots peers and their ladies. When George IV came in August, 1822, and held a levee at Holyrood, 63 peers paraded, followed by 77 baronets, and some 2,000 untitled gentlemen. Some of the Highland chiefs appeared with "tails" of men at arms in tartan kilts; and Sir Walter Scott, who stage-managed the visit, wore a kilt himself, of Campbell tartan for some female ancestress, and persuaded George IV to appear, twice, in a kilt of Stewart tartan. The portly monarch wore silk tights beneath it. The even portlier Lord Mayor of London wore a kilt too. At the peers' ball only reels and strathspeys and other national dances were performed; but the Caledonian Hunt added waltzes to theirs. A separate levee was held for ministers and elders of the kirk. At the annual levees of the King's High Commissioner to the General Assembly, a Scots peer, it was more or less socially obligatory for heads of landowning families, even if not Presbyterian, to show a leg, along with the rural ministers and elders, and the judges and advocates. The top-ranking lords and lairds might be members of the Royal Company of Archers, with its handsome uniform, and the not-quite-so-top men might be found in the corps of High Constables of Holyrood, founded in 1787. The parliamentary elections for the sixteen Scots representative peers were great social occasions, with much petticoat government in the background, dowagers intriguing for votes, where there were, as Lord Kinnaird put it, "more piglets than teats." The elected sixteen would give dinners or balls, one of which James Boswell describes. Peers were to be seen about the town wearing the broad ribbons and stars of orders they might possess, and they addressed one another as "Your Lordship" or "My Lord," until long after Scott's day. There were thousands of non-titled Scots related to these top persons, and very well aware of the cousinship, however remote: so that foreigners remarked a certain aristocratic tone in the behavior of professional and commercial men who in other countries would not have been so highly regarded socially.

The judges were accorded suitable respect, with a grain of

salt, even by themselves. Lord President Forbes proposed a toast: "Here's to such of the judges as don't deserve the gallows." Lord Kames, on leaving the bench, said, "Fare ye weel, ye bitches." And a certain frivolity kept intruding even from the bench. In sentencing to death one Matthew Hay, with whom he had played chess, Kames remarked: "That's checkmate to you, Mattha!" Presiding at the trial of Gerard, one of the Friends of the People, when the reformer observed that Jesus Christ had been a reformer too, Braxfield retorted: "Muckle he made o' that. He was hangit." Squabbles for precedence among officeholders broke out during a great fire near the Law Courts in 1824. Cockburn says it was "rather sternly discussed on the street whether the Lord Provost could order the Justice-Clerk to prison, or the Justice the Provost, and whether George Cranstoun, the Dean of the Faculty, was bound to work at an engine, when commanded by John Hope, the Solicitor-General, to do so, or *vice versa*."

The Advocates were the most characteristic body of Edinburgh society, with plenty of time on their hands. Soon after Scott's time there were no fewer than 462 members of the Faculty, of whom 92 were authors. Not many more than a dozen made good incomes from practice; the rest had inherited money or married it. There were also a good many army officers hanging about Edinburgh, either in the castle garrison, which numbered about 2,000 at maximum, or retired on half-pay. Those who had served in India looked down on the rest. By London standards, Edinburgh had no dandies; but these gentlemen of leisure ran the organized amusements, such as horse-racing on Leith sands; curling, if the winter brought enough cold for ice; golfing, in red coats, at Bruntsfield or Leith; and cockfighting. Duels were rare. Phrenology had a brief vogue.

Writers to the Signet and other lawyers had to keep office-hours, as did the merchants and shopkeepers. Early seekers of news would gather at the Cross at 7:00 A.M., and shops would open after breakfast at 8:00. Merchants did business in the open air, rather than at their Exchange. At 11:30 the bells of St. Giles would play tunes, and there would be a general exodus to the innumerable taverns for the first alcoholic drink of the day, apart from the small ale taken with the breakfast porridge. Shops shut from 12:00 until 2:00 for dinner, which in most homes was vegetable broth with oatcakes and cheese, sometimes meat on Sundays, and often fish. Vegetables were retailed by a sorority of gin-drinking old women round the Cross. A bell at 8:00 P.M. was the signal for shutting shops for the day, and tradesmen normally then spent an hour or two in a tavern. The innumerable clubs, whether for music or debate or literature or plain drinking, normally met in taverns (pubs). A roll of drums at 10:00 was the signal for shutting the taverns, and for emptying excreta from the windows: so that the home-going reveler often had to cry in alarm, "Haud your hand!"

The gentry dined at two or three o'clock around 1770, but about five or six o'clock later on. Formal dinners were boring by reason of the obligation for every diner to toast every other diner individually, and to propose sentiments, such as "Mair freends and less need o' them," or "Delicate pleasures to susceptible minds." Suppers were much preferred, as cheaper,

147

shorter, less ceremonious, and more poetical. Ladies held tea parties, between four and six, at one time with gentlemen present; the silver spoons were each numbered, to avoid confusion on refilling; and the etiquette was to leave the spoon in the cup, not in the saucer, when one wished no further supply. Cards often followed the tea. A coffeehouse had been opened in 1675, but tea was much more relished, often laced with whisky, which only cost 10*d*. a quart. Rum and sugar had come in from the 1680's. With sugar and lemons and hot water, fortified by rum, whisky, or brandy, a convivial group would brew a punch, and ladle it round the glasses. Scots silverwork had long been fine, and at this time became more abundant. The practice of destroying a glass after drinking a toast gradually went out.

In ordinary families supper was again porridge, and the appurtenances of the table were modest, usually just wooden bowls and cups and horn spoons. But the gentry enjoyed standards in plate, porcelain, foods, and wines as high as most in Europe. A Scots partiality was for five-year-old mutton and old claret, David Hume's favorite repast. John Home wrote an epigram on the shift from French claret to Portuguese port, occasioned by English political alliances:

> *Firm and erect the Caledonian stood;*
> *old was his mutton, and his claret good.*
> *"Let him drink port!" the Saxon statesman cried.*
> *He drank the poison, and his spirit died.*

The judge Lord Newton never did business without imbibing six pints of claret, and could keep as clear a head as need be. Jeffrey, in his country house at Craigcrook, held parties where dinner, at five, was preceded by a contest in long jumping, and thirty-two sorts of wine were on hand. He preferred champagne, which came in after 1815.

Edinburgh was fortunate in supplies of fresh seafish, and lobsters, oysters, and mussels. The fishermen's womenfolk were a remarkable breed. They could carry a hundredweight of wet fish many miles up country. Three of them were recorded as walking from Dunbar to Edinburgh, twenty-seven miles, each with a two-hundred-pound load. If the boats came in late, the Inveresk women would run the five miles to Edinburgh inside forty-five minutes, in relays, each carrying the basket one hundred yards, to get the fish to market in time for dinner. These women played at golf and football, and many of them were popular dancers. Fashionable folk from the New Town liked to spend an evening in a cellar night club of the Old Town, with oysters and porter, a strong type of beer, seeing the oyster-women dance. A raffish tone had been current even before the Regency. It was fashionable for ladies to be pretty free-spoken, and to use oaths. Hume remarks that in French *salons* there was "Scarce a double Entendre to be heard; scarce a free Joke." He solemnly defends "bawdy" to the Lord Advocate, writing: "I know not a more agreeable subject both for books and conversation, if executed with decency and ingenuity."

Edinburgh people were also great scandalmongers. Lord Kames picked up gossip every day from one "Sinkum the Cawdie," on his way to Court. This was a member of the fraternity of caddies, who hung about the Cross, to run er

149

rands. They knew everybody and everything, and helped to prevent crime accordingly. If one were ever dishonest, the fraternity made good his employer's loss.

There seems, indeed, to have been remarkably little crime in Edinburgh before the 1790's; but, as Creech remarked, "As opulence increases, virtue subsides." In 1805 an unarmed police was instituted. Previously, there had been a city guard of veteran soldiers, with Lochaber axes, a combination of spear, ax, and hook. The most sensational criminality was that of Burke and Hare, who in the 1820's murdered people to sell their corpses to anatomists. Scott reported in 1812 the discovery of "a formal association among nearly fifty apprentices aged from twelve to twenty to scour the streets and knock down and rob all whom they found in their way." They had been meeting for months, and keeping regular minutes; and executed their grand design on the last night of the year, hogmanay. But this specimen of concerted juvenile delinquency seems to be unique. On the other hand, mob violence broke out now and again, for instance, in 1779, in protest against the toleration of Roman Catholicism, when the historian Robertson's house was burned down; and in 1832, for the carrying of the Reform Bill, when a mob of thousands smashed the windows of Tories who would not light up to celebrate. The slogan was, "Up with Reform light! Down with Tory darkness!" Mudie comments on the diligence of artisans in attending evening classes, which he found made them more formidable as a mob when they chose to riot. This was part of the sharpening class conflict towards the end of Scott's life.

The licensed beggars were a privileged small group, with their blue gowns, and their purses, annually replenished by as many pence as the reigning king had years. There was a regulation sum to give them, and gentlemen who did not have it exact were not ashamed to ask change amounting to one-sixth of a penny. The afflux of unlicensed beggars from the countryside was resisted; but after 1825, when there was a general financial crisis, Edinburgh became full of unemployed building workers, and schemes of emergency poor relief had to be undertaken, as in 1795 and 1816. A distinct caste, too, were the sedan-chair carriers, mainly Gaelic-speakers; but the move to the New Town reduced them to vanishing point. Coal porters and water carriers were distinctive trades, requiring soundness of heart to carry loads up and down the tall common stairs of the tenements.

For wage earners in such industries as existed the hours of labor were long at bad times. Somerville worked in a saw pit from 6:00 A.M. to 7:00 P.M., living on porridge morning and night, and broth for dinner, with meat never and bread seldom. He drank *soor dook*, a raw kind of buttermilk; and spent his money on books and writing materials; he was one of an exceptionally able and aspiring minority among the underprivileged, but he observes that most Scottish soldiers could write and keep accounts, whereas few could do so in English or Irish regiments. The Shorter Catechism given by Presbyterians to their children often had the multiplication tables printed on the back, to rear a generation both godly and calculating.

Somerville describes his dress in 1831 as thick shoes, corduroy trousers, a fustian coat, and a blue bonnet. The upper ranks wore tail coats and top hats by then, having discarded breeches, cloaks, and three-cornered hats. At home at leisure they sat around in caps and nightgowns. Scott in his country house, at Abbotsford, dressed, says Cockburn, like a smuggler or a poacher. "His simplicity and naturalness after all his fame are absolutely incredible." In general foreigners seem to have been struck by the naturalness of Scottish behavior. Buzonnière notes that the Scots "have too much imagination to preserve the cold dignity of the English gentlemen." Though Oliver Goldsmith, in 1753, had found the Scots behaving at dances with "a formality approaching to despondence," Lockhart in the 1820's comments on Scots dancers "glorying in muscular agitation and alertness." The English Captain Topham found that "The air of mirth and vivacity, that quick penetrating look, that spirit of gaiety which distinguished the French, is equally visible in the Scotch." A London lady, Mrs. Elizabeth Montagu, notes that the Scots "live in ye french way, *des petits soupers fins*, & they have ye easy address of the french." Cobbett, writing from Edinburgh, states: ". . . better manners never were exhibited in this world than by my audiences here," and "Every man that I have met with at Edinburgh has been as kind to me as if he were my brother." Lockhart, an Anglicized snob of the type that became commoner after Scott's time, writes: "People visit each other in Edinburgh with all the appearance of cordial familiarity, who, if they lived in London, would imagine their differences of rank to form an impassable barrier against such intercourse."

It was precisely the habit of kindly intercourse among different income groups and occupational types that promoted the development of diverse talent in Edinburgh. William Smellie, editor of the first *Encyclopaedia Britannica*, quoted a comment of Mr. Amyat, the King's chemist, who had resided in Edinburgh a year or two: "Here I stand at what is called the *Cross of Edinburgh*, and can, in a few minutes, take fifty men of genius and learning by the hand. . . . In Edinburgh, the access of men of parts is not only easy, but their conversation and the communication of their knowledge are at once imparted to intelligent strangers with the utmost liberality. The philosophers of Scotland have no nostrums. They tell what they know, and deliver their sentiments without disguise or reserve." Mudie remarks that the people of "the modern Athens" had "gusto, and grace, and gravity." It must have been a most exciting city to live in, with Walter Scott and so many more as fellow citizens.

Selected Bibliography

WORKS ON SCOTTISH HISTORY AND INSTITUTIONS:

Craik, Sir Henry. *A Century of Scottish History*. 2nd ed. Edinburgh, 1911.

Dickinson, William Croft, and George S. Pryde. *A New History of Scotland*. 2 parts. London, 1961–62.

Fergusson of Kilkerran, Sir James. *The Sixteen Peers of Scotland*. Oxford, 1960.

Furber, Holden. *Henry Dundas, First Viscount Melville, 1742–1811: Political Manager of Scotland, Statesman, Administrator of British India*. London, 1931.

Gaskin, Maxwell. *The Scottish Banks*. London, 1965.

Hamilton, Henry. *An Economic History of Scotland in the Eighteenth Century*. Oxford, 1963.

Mackie, John D. *A History of Scotland*. Baltimore, 1964.

Mathieson, William Law. *The Awakening of Scotland: A History from 1747 to 1797*. Glasgow, 1910.

Meikle, Henry W. *Scotland and the French Revolution*. Glasgow, 1912.

Plant, Marjorie. *The Domestic Life of Scotland in the Eighteenth Century*. Edinburgh, 1952.

Reid, J.M. *Kirk and Nation: The Story of the Reformed
Church of Scotland*. London, 1960.

Saunders, Laurence James. *Scottish Democracy, 1815–1840:
The Social and Intellectual Background*. Edinburgh, 1950.

Smith, T.B. *The United Kingdom: The Development of Its
Laws and Constitutions; Scotland*. London, 1955.

WORKS ON EDINBURGH:

Book of the Old Edinburgh Club, The. Vol. I (Edinburgh,
1908) to Vol. XXXI (1962).

Chambers, Robert. *Traditions of Edinburgh*. Edinburgh,
1955.

Cockburn, Henry. *Memorials of His Time*. Edinburgh, 1910.

Heiton, John. *The Castes of Edinburgh*. Edinburgh, 1859.

Lindsay, Ian G. *Georgian Edinburgh*. Edinburgh, 1948.

Lockhart, John Gibson. *Peter's Letters to His Kinsfolk*. 3rd.
ed. 3 vols. Edinburgh, 1819.

Mudie, Robert. *The Modern Athens: A Dissection and Dem-
onstration of Men and Things in the Scotch Capital, by a
Modern Greek*. London, 1825.

Royal Scottish Geographical Society, The. *The Early Views
and Maps of Edinburgh, 1544–1852*. Edinburgh, 1919.

Scott-Moncrieff, George. *Edinburgh*. London, 1947. Second
edition, 1964.

Stuart, Marie W. *Old Edinburgh Taverns*. London, 1952.

Works on Scottish Sciences, Arts, and Letters:

Carlyle, Alexander. *The Autobiography of Dr. Alexander Carlyle of Inveresk, 1722–1805*. Edinburgh, 1910.

Clement, A.G., and R.H.S. Robertson. *Scotland's Scientific Heritage*. Edinburgh, 1961.

Clive, John. *Scotch Reviewers: The* Edinburgh Review, *1802–1815*. London, 1957.

Craig, David. *Scottish Literature and the Scottish People, 1680–1830*. London, 1961.

Cursiter, Stanley. *Scottish Art to the Close of the Nineteenth Century*. London, 1949.

Daiches, David. *The Paradox of Scottish Culture: The Eighteenth-Century Experience*. London, 1964.

Davie, George Elder. *The Democratic Intellect: Scotland and Her Universities in the Nineteenth Century*. Edinburgh, 1961.

Farmer, Henry George. *A History of Music in Scotland*. London, 1947.

Fleming, John. *Robert Adam and His Circle in Edinburgh and Rome*. London, 1962.

Grant, Sir Alexander. *The Story of the University of Edinburgh*. 2 vols. London, 1884.

Grave, S.A. *The Scottish Philosophy of Common Sense*. Oxford, 1960.

Hancock, P.D. *A Bibliography of Books Relating to Scotland, 1916–1950*. Two parts. Edinburgh, 1959–60.

Kinsley, James (editor). *Scottish Poetry: A Critical Survey*. London, 1955.

Mossner, Ernest Campbell. *The Life of David Hume*. Edinburgh, 1954.

Ramsay of Ochtertyre, John. *Scotland and Scotsmen in the Eighteenth Century*. 2 vols. Edinburgh, 1888.

Smart, Alastair. *The Life and Art of Allan Ramsay*. London, 1952.

Somerville, Thomas. *My Own Life and Times, 1741–1814*. Edinburgh, 1816.

Wittig, Kurt. *The Scottish Tradition in Literature*. Edinburgh, 1958.

BIBLIOGRAPHIES:

The best bibliographies may be found in issues of *The Scottish Historical Review* since 1904.

Index

128ff., 131 ff., 146; educational background of, 113; *see also* dramatists, historians

Baillie, Lady Grizell: 111
Baird, Rev. George Husband: 66
Balfour, Arthur James, Earl of Balfour: 23
Baliol (Balliol), John de, king of Scotland: 9f.
Ballantyne, James: 126f.
Bank of Scotland: 21
Banks, Scottish: 21–22; merchant banking, 22; savings bank movement, 22
Bannockburn, Scotland: battle of, 10, 58
Barbour, John: 116
Barclay de Tolly, Mikhail, Prince: 24
Barrie, Sir James Matthew: 108
Barrow, Professor G.W.S.: 9
Bastards: fines for, 74
Beattie, Professor James: 61
Beethoven, Ludwig van: 108, 110
Beggars: 151
Bell, Andrew: 135
Bell, Sir Charles: 82
Bellarmine, Cardinal Robert: 66
Berlin, Sir Isaac: 96
Bishops: 8ff., 13f., 43, 76
Black, Joseph: 81, 132
"Black Watch, The" (regiment): 24, 131
Blacklock, Mr.: *Poems by Mr. Blacklock,* 116
Blackstone, Sir William: 47
Blackwood's Magazine: 113, 139–40, 141; *Noctes Ambrosianae,* 139–40
Blair, Rev. Dr. Hugh: 114, 118f.; on Hume's skepticism, 61

Blair, Robert (of Avontown): 53–54
Blane of Blanefield, Gilbert: 86
Boece, Hector: 116
Boswell, James: 34, 44, 51, 53, 120, 145
Bower, Alice (Mrs. John Ramsay): 104
Brewster, Sir David: 86–87
Bridie, James: 108
British Association for the Advancement of Science: 87
British Linen Bank: 21
The Briton: 23
Brodie, Deacon William: 142
Brothels: 74, 105, 141
Brougham, Henry Peter, Baron: 63, 136
Broun, Samuel: 22
Brown, John: 87
Brown (of Montrose), Robert: 89
Bruce, Charles, Earl of Elgin: 37, 99
Bruce, Robert de VI, Lord Annandale: 10
Bruce, Robert de (Robert I), king of Scotland: 9f., 31, 58, 105; daughter Marjorie, 15
Bruce family: 8
Brühl, Gräfin: 124–25
Buchanan, Dugald: 129
Buchanan, George: 66, 116f.
Bürger, Gottfried August: *Lenore,* 124
Burghers (Presbyterian sect): 70
Burke, William: 150
Burnet, Sir Thomas: *Thesaurus Medicinae,* 79
Burns, Robert: *ix, xi,* 7, 22, 29, 35, 54, 57, 69, 102, 105, 107–108, 109ff., 112, 123, 127, 131, 143; monument to, 37; *The Holy Fair,* 67; *Holy Willie's Prayer,* 75; head

Index

Ferguson, James: 87
Ferguson, William Gouw: 89
Ferguson of Pitfour: 53
Ferguson, Colonel Patrick, of Pitfour: 85
Fergusson, George, Lord Hermand: 76
Fergusson, Robert: 110, 121
Fielding, Henry: 123
Fife, hills of (Scotland): 31
Fingal (Celtic epic): 23, 119
Finlay, George: 143
Firth of Forth, Scotland: 28, 112
Fish-wives: 149
Fletcher, Andrew: 55
Food and dining: 145, 147–48, 149, 151
Forbes, Anne: 94
Forbes, Duncan: 145
Forbes, James David: 89
Forbes, Sir William: 124
Fornication: 73–74
Forsyth, Rev. Alexander John: 85
Forth River, Scotland: 3, 5, 86, 94, 129; estuary of, 31
Foulis, Andrew: 97
Foulis, Robert: 97
Foulis, Sir James, of Woodhall: 102
France: 12, 18, 20, 51, 93, 97f., 113, 130; alliance with Scotland, 10, 12, 18, 24, 51
Franklin, Benjamin: 29
Frazer, Major Andrew: 36
Frederick II (Frederick the Great), king of Prussia: 24
Frederick Louis, prince of Wales: 23
Free Church of Scotland (Presbyterian): 77f., 141
French Revolution: Scottish sympathizers, 54f.

Friends of the People: *see* Society of Friends of the People
Fuseli, Henry: 93

Gaelic (language): 5ff., 18, 119, 128f.; Scots-Gaelic dictionary, 128
Galt, John: 113, 128
Garden, Francis, Lord Gardenstone: 102
Gay, John: 107
Ged, William: 88
Geddes, Andrew: 97
General Associate Synod: 46
Geologists: *see* scientists
George II, king of Great Britain: 97
George III, king of Great Britain: 23, 92, 99f.
George IV, king of Great Britain: 37, 71, 95, 97, 144
Gerrald (Gerard), Joseph: 146
Gibbon, Edward: 118
Gibbs, James: 98
Gladstone, William Ewart: 23, 33
Glasgow, Scotland: 8, 21 f., 27, 50, 54
Godwin, William: 138
Goethe, Johann Wolfgang von: 23, 94, 111; *Götz von Berlichingen*, 125
Goldsmith, Oliver: 152
Goodall, Walter: 117
Goodsir, John: 82
Gow, Nathaniel: 111
Gow, Niel: 111
Graham, Ian C.C.: *Colonists from Scotland,* 29
Graham, Thomas: 89
Graham, Thomas, Baron Lynedoch: 118
Graham family: 8
Gray, Agnes (Lord Byron's nurse): 143

163

Greenshields, Rev. James: 44
Gregory, Duncan Farquharson: 80
Gregory, James: 80
Gregory family: 80
Guns, naval: contracts for, 28

Hall, Sir James, of Dunglass: 84
Hamilton, Sir William: 133
Hamilton, Gavin, of Murdostoun: 91
Handfasting: 51
Hare, William: 150
Hay, Matthew: 146
Hayden, Franz Joseph: 108, 110
Hellenism: 36–37, 99
Heriot, George: 95
High Constables of Holyrood: 145
Highfliers: 65
Highland Society of Scotland: 37
Highlanders: 25, 34
Historians: 115ff., 118
Hogg, James: 75, 143
Home, Francis: 83
Home, Henry, Lord Kames: 65, 92, 146, 149
Home, Rev. John: 65, 118, 148; *Douglas*, 65, 109, 116
Hope, Charles: 98
Hope, John: 81, 146
Hope, John, Earl of Hopetoun: 98, 103f.
Hope, Thomas Charles: 81
Hope family: 20
Horner, Francis: 63, 136
Howard, John: 117
Hume, David: *ix*ff., 8, 19, 29, 32, 34f., 44, 46f., 52, 63, 65, 80, 84, 90–91, 92, 104, 108f., 113, 115f., 118, 120, 123, 129f., 148f.; skepticism of, 61–62, 63; causation theory, 62f., 75; attacked in General Assembly (1756), 65

Hume, Joseph, Laird of Ninewalls: 19
Hume family: 8
Hunter, William: 82
Hutcheson, Francis: 130
Hutton, James: 83–84
Hygienists: 86f.

Innes, Thomas: 117
Innes, Sir Thomas, of Learney: 25
Institution for the Encouragement of the Fine Arts: 96
Inventors: 85ff., 88f., 102
Inveresk, Scotland: 65; women of, 149
Inverness, Scotland: 5, 20
Iona (island): 5
Ireland: 4f., 54, 56, 68, 101, 133; universities in, 78
Isles, Scottish: 5, 118, 138
Italy: 12, 89ff., 93, 97, 100, 132

James III, king of Scotland: 12
James IV, king of Scotland: 12
James V, king of Scotland: 12, 105
James VI, king of Scotland: 12, 14, 42, 106
James VII, king of Scotland (James II of England): 15
Jamesone, George: 89
Jamieson, Dr. John: *Etymological Dictionary of the Scottish Language,* 128
Jardine, James: 86
Jeffrey, Francis, Lord: 63, 136–37, 141; Craigcrook (parties at), 149
John Coutts and Company: 22
Johnson, Samuel: 34, 45, 90, 92, 120, 129, 134
Johnstone, James, Marquis of Annandale: 90, 98, 129

Jones, John Paul: 30, 38–39
Journalists: 116, 132, 136ff.
Judges: 20, 33, 52ff., 109, 117, 121,
    137, 141, 145–46; Commissioners
    of Justiciary, 50
Jury trial, civil: 50
Jacobites: 15, 24–25, 37, 44, 59, 79,
    131; 1745 Rising, 24, 29, 54, 112,
    117, 126

Kay, John: 94
Keith, James Francis Edward: 24
King's College, Aberdeen, Scotland:
    12, 63
Kinnaird, Lord: 145
Kintyre Peninsula, Scotland: 5
Knox, John: 13, 108; *First Book of
    Discipline*, 43

Laborers: 151
Lairds: *see* nobility
Lanarkshire, Scotland: 46, 103f.
Lapsie, James, of Campsie: 70–71
Law, Bonar: 23
Law: Scots, 7, 16f., 47ff., 51ff., 64,
    123; Roman, 19, 47, 51, 123;
    English, 21, 52; feudal, 47; civil,
    51; Celtic, 51
Lawyers: *x*, 19ff., 28, 46, 50f., 84,
    134; solicitors, 52; law agents, 52;
    Writers to His Majesty's Signet, 52,
    147; advocates, 52, 145f.
Leiden, University of (The Nether-
    lands): 19, 51, 79, 83
Leith, Scotland: 19, 27, 36, 38, 82,
    146f.; ship industry in, 38, 86;
    transportation in, 38
Leslie, James, Count: 95
Leslie, Sir John: 75f., 87
Lewis, Matthew Gregory ("Monk"):
    125

Libraries: 106–107, 123, 136
Lighthouses: 82
Lind, Dr. James: 85f.
Lindsay, Lady Anne: 39, 111
Lindsay, Sir David: 105
Lindsay, Ian: *Georgian Edinburgh*,
    37
Lindsay family: 8
Lockhart, John Gibson: 70, 133, 152
London, England: 24, 37, 56, 89ff.,
    94f., 97, 99, 101f., 106f., 111f.,
    119, 124f., 135, 152; trans-Atlan-
    tic trade in, 27; transportation to,
    38, Spencer House 99; removal of
    Scots Parliament to, 103, 106
Lord Advocate: 51, 53, 55
Louis XVI, king of France: 56
The Lounger (periodical): 129
Lyell, Sir Charles: 84

Mabillon, Jean: 116
MacAdam, John Loudon: 87
MacAlpin, Kenneth, king of the
    Scots: 5, 15
Macaulay, Thomas Babington, Baron
    Macaulay of Rothley: 137
Macbeth, king of Scotland: 6
MacCodrum, John: 129
McCulloch, Rev. William: 46
Macdonald, Flora: 30
Macdonald, Jacques Étienne Joseph
    Alexandre, Duke of Tarenti: 24
MacDonald, James Ramsay: 23
Macfarquhar, Colin: 135
Macintosh, Charles: 88
Macintyre, Duncan Ban: 128
Mackay, Rob Donn: 129
Mackenzie, Henry: 123, 126
Mackenzie, Sir George Stewart, of
    Coull: 84
Macknight, Rev. Dr.: 75

Maclaurin, Colin: 86

Macmillan, Harold: 23

MacMillan, Kirkpatrick: 89

Macpherson, James: 23, 118–20, 123; *Ossian*, 100

Macqueen, Robert, Lord Braxfield: at Thomas Muir's trial, 56–57, 58

Maitland, James, Earl of Lauderdale: 54, 76

Marat, Jean Paul: 79

Margaret, of Scotland (queen and patron saint of Scotland): 6, 8, 94

Margarot, Maurice: 57

Marischal College, Aberdeen, Scotland: 12, 23

Marriage: 51

Marshall, Henry: 86

Martin, David: 95

Mary II (joint British sovereign with William III): 15

Mary of Guise (queen of James V of Scotland): 12f.

Mary Stuart, Queen of Scots: 12, 96–97, 105, 117

Mathematicians: *see* scientists

Medical men: *see* doctors

Meikle, Andrew: 21

Meikle Ballrch Hill, Scotland: 3

Melville, Andrew: 42

Melville, General Robert: 85

Merchants: 19f., 27, 33f., 84, 130, 147

Mill, James: 63

Millar, William: 93

Millar of Dalswinton, Patrick: 101

Ministers and ministry: x, 6f., 13f., 19f., 42ff., 45f., 55, 63ff., 66, 68, 69–72, 73, 75, 85, 102, 111, 134, 118, 145; appointment of, 45, 64, 77; maxims for, 60–61; status of,

68–69; revolt of (in Church of Scotland), 77

The Mirror, Edinburgh: 114, 129

Moncreiff, Rev. Sir Henry: 71–72, 76

Monro, Alexander: 79f.

Monro, Alexander (the Second): 80

Montagu, Lord: 69

Montagu, Mrs. Elizabeth (Robinson): 152

Moore, G. E.: 64

Moore, General Sir John: 88

Moore, Thomas: 138

Moray, Sir Andrew: 10

More, Jacob: 94

Morton, Thomas: 86

Mossner, Ernest Campbell: on Hume's causation theory, 62

Mounier, J.J.: 138

Mudie, Robert: 139, 142, 150, 153; on Edinburgh, 140–41

Muir, Thomas, of Huntershill: 55–58; trial for sedition, 54, 56ff., 59

Murdock, William: 87–88

Murray, John: 139

Murray family: 8

Music, Scottish: 108, 110–11

Music and musical instruments: 107f., 110–11

Musical Society of Edinburgh: 110

Mylne, Robert: 101

Mylne, Thomas: 101

Mylne, William: 101

Nairne, Carolina (Oliphant), Baroness: 77, 111

Napier, Macvey: 135

Napier family: 20

Napoleon I, emperor of the French: 23f., 85, 135

Nasmyth, Alexander: 101–102

Nasmyth, James: 89, 102

Reid, Robert: 36

Reid, Thomas: 63

Relief (Presbyterian sect): 70

Rennie, John: 86

Revett, Nicholas: *Antiquities of Athens*, 98–99

Richardson, Samuel: 123

Robert I, king of Scotland: *see* Bruce, Robert de

Robertson, William: 68, 115, 136, 150

Robison, John: 86

Rodney, George Brydges, Baron: 85

Roman Catholic church (in Scotland): 8f., 37, 70; bishops of, 8ff.; decline of, 12ff.; parishes, 43

Romans: 3f.

Ross, Christian (Mrs. Allan Ramsay [poet]): 104

Ross, William: 129

Royal Bank of Scotland: 21

Royal College of Physicians of Edinburgh: 79

Royal College of Surgeons, Edinburgh: 79

Royal Company of Archers, Edinburgh: 121, 145

Royal Scottish Academy: 96

Royal Society of Edinburgh: 80, 86, 133

Ruddiman, Thomas: 104, 116–17

Ruddiman, Thomas (the Younger): 117

Ruddiman, Walter: 117

Runciman, Alexander: 91, 93–94; paintings in Penicuik House, 91, 93–94

Russell, John, Earl: 63

Rutherford, Anne (Mrs. Walter Scott): 122

Rutherford, Daniel: 81

Salisbury Crags, Edinburgh: 32

Sark River: 6

Scientists: *x*, 80–81, 82ff., 85ff., 88f.; *see also* inventors

Scotland: 3ff., 6f., 11 ff., 14ff., 18, 22, 24ff., 55f., 58, 80, 83, 89, 91, 100, 104, 107f., 110f., 113, 116f., 120f., 130, 133f., 140, 143, 153; languages in, 7–8, 18; alliance with France (*Auld Alliance*), 10, 12, 18, 24, 51; foreign influences on, 12; union of Scots and English parliaments, 16, 25, 27, 30, 44f., 52, 68, 89, 103, 116 (*see also* Treaty of Union, 1707); agricultural revolution and land improvement in, 18f., 20–21, 22, 27; population of, 19; depopulation of, 24, 27; Highlands of, 24, 54, 68, 118, 120, 131, 138; borders of, 27, 118, 124f.; Commerce and industry in, 27–28; political management of, 28; nationalism in, 48–49; Lord Advocate in, 53; government in, 58–60; Lowlands of, 68; removal of royal court and Parliament, 90, 115; doctrine of Free Trade in, 130

Scots (Gaelic tribe): 4–5, 8, 15; arrival in Scotland, 5

Scots (language): 7, 18, 104, 105–106, 113f., 118, 120ff., 125f., 127–28, 129, 140; Court Scots ("Broad Scotch" or "Lallans"), 7, 28, 99; Scots-Gaelic dictionary, 128

Scotsman (newspaper): 68

Scott, Charles: 69

Scott, Henry, Duke of Buccleuch: 29, 69, 124f., 129